All of my Anxieties Under One Cover

All of my Anxieties Under One Cover

James Earl Cox III

ISBN: 978-1-7365051-3-7

DEDICATION

There is too much to do and too little time.

CONTENTS

ACKNOWLEDGMENTS

I acknowledge that I bit off more than I could chew. If there are any spelling, or formatting, or grammatical errors, I am sorry. I didn't have enough time.

I DO NOT HAVE TIME FOR THIS

I do not have time for this.

I do not have time for this.

I do not have time for this. I do not have

time for this. I do not have time for this. I do not have time for this. I do not have time for this. I do not have time for this. I do not have time for this. I do not have time for this. I do not have time for this. I do not have time for this. I do not have time for this. I do not have time for this. I do not have time for this. I do not have time for this. I do not have time for this. I do not have time for this. I do not have time for this. I do not have time for this. I do not have time for this. I do not have time for this.

I do not have time for this. I do not have time for this. I do not have time for this. I do not have time for this. I do not have time for this. I do not have time for this. I do not have time for this. I do not have time for this. I do not have time for this. I do not have time for this. I do not have time for this. I do not have time for this. I do not have time for this. I do not have time for this. I do not have time for this. I do not have time for this. I do not have time for this.

I do not have time for this. I do not have time for this. I do not have time for this. I do not have time for this. I do not have time for this. I do not have time for this. I do not have time for this. I do not have time for this. I do not have time for this. I do not have time for this. I do not have time for this. I do not have time for this. I do not have time for this.

I do not have time for this. I do not have time for this. I do not have time for this. I do not have time for this.

I do not have time for this. I do not have time for this. I do not have time for this. I do not have time for this. I do not have time for this. I do not have time for this. I do not have time for

this. I do not have time for this. I do not have time for this. I do not have time for this. I do not have time for this. I do not have time for this. I do not have time for this. I do not have time for this.

I do not have time for this. I do not have time for this.

I do not have time for this. I do not have time for this.

I do not have time for this. I do not have time for this. I do

not have time for this. I do not have time for this.

I do not have time for this. I do not have time for this. I do not have time for this. I do not have time for this. I do not have time for this. I do not have time for this. I do not have time for this. I do not have time for this. I do not have time for this. I do not have time for this. I do not have time for this. I do not have time for this. I do not have time for this. I do not have time for this.

I do not have time for this. I do not have time for this. I do not have time for this. I do not have time for this. I do not have time for this. I do not have time for this. I do not have time for this. I do not have time for this. I do not have time for this. I do not have time for this.

I do not have time for this.

I do not have time for this. I do not have time for this. I do not have time for this. I do not have time for this. I do not have time for this. I do not have time for this. I do not have time for this. I do not have time for this. I do not have time for this. I do not have time for this.

I do not have time for this. I do not have time for this. I do not have time for this. I do not have time for this. I do not have time for this. I do not have time for this. I do not have time for this. I do not have time for this.

I do not have time for this. I do not have time for this. I do not have time for this. I do not have time for this. I do not have

time for this.

I do not have time for this. I do not have time for this. I do not have time for this.

I do not have time for this. I do not have time for this. I do not have time for this.

I do not have time for this. I do not have time for this. I do not have time for this. I do not have time for this.

I do not have time for this. I do not have time for this. I do not have time for this. I do not have time for this.

I do not have time for this. I do not have time for this. I do not have time for this. I do not have time for this. I do not have time for this.

I do not have time for this. I do not have time for this. I do not have time for this. I do not have time for this. I do not have time for this.

I do not have time for this. I do not have time for this. I do not have time for this. I do not have time for this. I do not have time for this. I do not have time for this.

I do not have time for this. I do not have time for this. I do not have time for this. I do not have time for this. I do not have time for this. I do not have time for this.

I do not have time for this. I do not have time for this. I do not have time for this. I do not have time for this. I do not have

time for this. I do not have time for this. I do not have time for this. I do not have time for this. I do not have time for this. I do not have time for this. I do not have time for this. I do not have time for this. I do not have time for this.

I do not have time for this. I do not have time for this. I do not have time for this. I do not have time for this. I do not have time for this. I do not have time for this. I do not have time for this.

I do not have time for this. I do not have time for this. I do not have time for this. I do not have time for this. I do not have time for this. I do not have time for this.

I do not have time for this. I do not have time for this. I do not have time for this. I do not have time for this. I do not have time for this.

I do not have time for this. I do not have time for this. I do not have time for this. I do not have time for this.

I do not have time for this. I do not have time for this. I do not have time for this.

I do not have time for this. I do not have time for this.

I do not have time for this.

I do not have time for this. I do not have time for this. I do not have time for this. I do not have time for this. I do not have time for this. I do not have time for this. I do not have time for this. I do not have time for this. I do not have time for this. I do not have time for this. I do

not have time for this. I do not have time for this. I do

not have time for this. I do not have time for this. I do not have time for this. I do not have time for this. I do not have time for this. I do not have time for this. I do not have time for this. I do not have time for this.

I

do

not

have

time

for

this.

I do not have time for this. I do

not have time for thi

s. I do not have time for this. I do not have time for th

is. I do not have time for this. I do not have time for t

his. I do not have time for this. I do not have time fo

r this. I do not have time for this. I do not have time f

or this. I do not have time for this. I do not have tim

e for this. I do not have time for this. I do not have ti

me for this. I do not have time for this. I do not have t

ime for this. I do not have time for this. I do not hav

e time for this. I do not have time for this. I do not ha

ve time for this. I do not have time for this. I do not h

ave time for this. I do not have time for this. I do no

t have time for this. I do not have time for this. I do n

ot have time for this. I do not have time for this. I d

o not have time for this. I do not have time for this. I

do not have time for this. I do not have time for this. I do not have time for this. I do not have time for this. I do not have time for this. I do not have time for this. I do not have time for

this. I do not have time for this. I do not have time for this. I do not have time for this. I do not have time for this. I do not have time for this. I do not have time for this. I do not have time for this. I do not have time for this. I do not have time for this. I do not have time for this. I do not have time for this. I do not have time for this. I do not have time for this. I do not have time for this. I do not have time for this. I d

o n

ot h

ave t

ime f

or t

his. I do not have time for this. I do not have time for

this. I do not have time for this. I do not have time for this. I do not have time for this. I do not have time for this. I do not have time for this. I do not have time for this. I do not have time for this. I do not have time for this. I do not have time for this. I do not have time for this. I do not have time for this. I didn't ask for this.

I do not have time for this. I do not have time for this.

I do

not have

time for

this.

I do not have time for this. I do not have time for this. I do not have time for this. I do not have time for this.

I do not have time for this. I do not have time for this

I do not have time for this. I do not have time for this.

I do not have time for this. I do not have time for this.

I do not have time for this. I do not have time for this.

I do not have time for this. I do not have time for this.

I do not have time for this. I do not have time for this.

I do not have time for this. I do not have time for this.

I do not have time for this. I do not have time for this.

I do not have time for this. I do not have time for this.

I do not have time for this. I do not have time for this.

I do not have time for this. I do not have time for this.

I do not have time for this. I do not have time for this.

I do not have time for this. I do not have time for this.

I do not have time for this. I do not have time for this.

I do not have time for this. I do not have time for this.

I do not have time for this. I do not have time for this.

I do not have time for this. I do not have time for this.

I do not have time for this. I do not have time for this. I do not have time for this.

I do not have time for this. I do not have time for this. I do not have time for this.

I do not have time for this. I do not have time for this. I do not have time for this.

I do not have time for this. I do not have time for this. I do not have time for this.

I do not have time for this. I do not have time for this. I do not have time for this.

I do not have time for this. I do not have time for this. I do not have time for this.

I do not have time for this. I do

not have time for this. I do not have time for this. I do not have time for this. I do not have time for this. I do not have time for this. I do not have time for this.

I do not have time for this. I do not have time for this. I do not have time for this. I do not have time for this. I do not have time for this. I do not have time for this. I do not have time for this. I do not have time for this. I do not have time for this. I do not have time for this. I do not have time for this. I do not have time for this. I do not have time for this. I do not have time for this.

I do not have time for this. I do not have time for this. I do not have time for this. I do not have time for this. I do not have time for this. I do not have time for this. I do not have time for this. I do not have time for this. I do not have time for this. I do not have time for this. I do not have time for this. I do not have time for this. I do not have time for this. I do not have time for this.

I do not have time for this. I do not have time for this.

I do not have time for this.

I do not have time for this. I do not have time for this.

I do not have time for this. I do not have time for this. I do not have time for this.

I do not have time for this. I do not have time for this. I do not have time for this. I do not have time for this.

I do not have time for this. I do not have time for this. I do not have time for this. I do not have time for this. I do not have time for this.

I do not have time for this. I do not have time for this. I do not have time for this. I do not have time for this. I do not have time for this. I do not have time for this.

I do not have time for this. I do not have time for this. I do not have time for this. I do not have time for this. I do not have time for this. I do not have time for this. I do not have time for this.

I do not have time for this. I do not have time for this. I do not have time for this. I do not have time for this. I do not have time for this. I do not have time for this. I do not have time for this. I do not have time for this.

I do not have time for this. I do not have time for this. I do not have time for this. I do not have time for this. I do not have time for this. I do not have time for this. I do not have time for this. I do not have time for this. I do not have time for this.

I do not have time for this. I do not have time for this. I do not have time for this. I do not have time for this. I do not have time for this. I do not have time for this. I do not have time for this. I do not have time for this. I do not have time for this. I do not have time for this. I do not have time for this. I do not have time for this. I do not have time for this.

I do not have time for this. I do not have time for this. I do not have time for this.

I do not have time for this. I do not have time for this.

I do not have time for this. I do not have time for this. I do not have time for this. I do not have time for this. I do not have time for this. I do not have time for this. I do not have time for this. I do not have time for this. I do not have time for this. I do not have time for this. I do not have time for this. I do not have time for this. I do not have time for this. I do not have time for this. I do not have time for this. I do not have time for this. I do not have time for this. I do not have time for this. I do not have time for this. I do not have time for this.

I do not have time for this.

I do not have time for this.

I do not have time for this.

I do not have time for this.

I do not have time for this.

I do not have time for this.

I do not have time for this.

I do not have time for this.

I do not have time for this. I do not have time for this.

I do not have time for this. I do not have time for this. I do not have time for this. I do not have time for this.

I do not have time for this. I do not have time for this. I do not have time for this. I do not have time for this. I do not have time for this. I do not have time for this. I do not have time for this. I do not have time for this. I do not have time for this. I do not have time for this. I do not have time for this. I do not have time for this. I do not have time for

this. I do not have time for this. I do not have time for this. I do not have time for this. I do not have time for this. I do not have time for this. I do not have time for this. I do not have time for this. I do not have time for this. I do not have time for this. I do not have time for this. I do not have time for this. I do not have time for this. I do

not

have time for this. I do not have time for this. I do not have time for this. I do not have time for this. I do not have time for this. I do not have time for this. I do not have time for this. I do

not

have time for this. I do not have time for this. I do not have time for this. I do not have time for this. I do not have time for this. I do not have time for this. I do not have time for this. I do

not

have time for this. I do not have time for this. I do not have time for this. I do not have time for this. I do not have time for this. I do not have time for this. I do

not

have time for this. I do not have time for this. I do not have time for this. I do not have time for this. I do not have time for this. I do

not

have time for this. I do

not

have time for this. I do not have time for this. I do not have time for this. I do not have time for this. I do not have time for this. I do not have time for this.

I do not

have time for this. I do not have time for this. I do not have time for this. I do not have time for this. I do not have time for this. I do not have time for this.

I do not

have time for this. I do not have time for this. I do not have time for this. I do not have time for this. I do not have time for this. I do not have time for this.

I do not

have time for this. I do not have time for this.

I do not

have time for this.

I do not

have time for this. I do not have time for this. I do not

have time for this. I do not have time for this.

I do not have time for this. I do not have time for this. I do not have time for this. I do not have time for this. I do not have time for this.

I definitely do not have time for this.

I do not have time for this. I do not have time for this.

I

do

not

have

time f

or this.

I do not h

ave time f

or this. I do

not have tim

e for this. I do

not have time f

or this. I do not h

ave time for this.

I do not have time f

or this. I do not have t

ime for this. I do not h

ave time for this. I do not have time for this.

I do not have time for this. I do not have time for this. I do not have time for this. I do not have time for this. I do not have time for this. I do not have time for this. I do not have time for this. I do not have time for this. I do not have time for this. I do not have time for this. I do not have time for this. I do not have

time for this. I do not have time for this. I do not have time for this. I do not have time for this. I do not have time for this. I do not have time for this. I do not have time for this.

I do not have time for this. I do not have time for this. I do

not have time for this. I do not have time for this. I do not have time for this. I do not have time for this. I do not have time for this. I do not have time for this. I

do not have time for this. I do not have time for this. I do not have time for this. I do not have time for this. I do not have time for this. I do not have time for this. I do not have

time for this. I do not have time for this. I do not have time for this. I do not have time for this. I do not

have time for this. I do not have time for this. I do not have time for this. I do not have time for this. I do not have time for this. I do not have time for this. I do not have time for this.

I d

o not ha

ve time for

this. I do not

have time for this. I d

o not have time for thi

s. I do not have time for this. I

do not have time for this. I do not hav

e time for this. I do not have time for th

is. I do not have time for this. I do not have t

ime for this. I do not have time for this. I do not have

time for this. I do not have time for this. I do not

have time for this. I do not have time for this.

I do not have time for this. I do not have t

ime for this. I do not have time for this.

I do not have time for this. I do not h

ave time for this. I do not have tim

e for this. I do not have time for

this. I do not have time for t

his. I do not have time for t

his. I do not have time for

this. I do not have time f

or this. I do not have

time for this. I do n

ot have time fo

r this. I do n

ot have

time for this.

I do not have time for this.

I do not have time for this. I do not have time for this.

I do not have time for this.

I do not have time for this. I do not have time for this.

I do not have time for this.

I do not have time for this. I do not have time for this.

I do not have time for this.

I do not have time for this. I do not have time for this.

I do not have time for this.

I do not have time for this. I do not have time for this.

I do not have time for this.

I do not have time for this. I do not have time for this.

I do not have time for this.

I do not have time for this. I do not have time for this.

I do not have time for this.

I do not have time for this. I do not have time for this.

I do not have time for this. I do not have time for this. I do not have time for this. I do not have time for this. I do not have time for this. I do not have time for this. I do not have time for this. I do not have time for this. I do not have time for this. I do not have time for this.

I do not have time for this. I do not have time for this. I do not have time for this. I do not have time for this. I do not have time for this. I do not have time for this. I do not have time for this. I do not have time for this. I do not have time for this. I do not have time for this. I do not have time for this. I do not have time for this. I do not have time for this.

I do not have time for this. I do not have time for this. I do not have time for this. I do not have time for this. I do not have time for this. I do not have time for this. I do not have time for this. I do not have time for this. I do not have time for this. I do not have time for this. I do not have time for this. I do not have time for this. I do not have time for this. I do not have time for this. I do not have time for this. I do not have time for this. I do not have time for this. I do not have time for this.

I do not have time for this. I do not have time for this. I do not have time for this. I do not have time for this. I do not have time for this. I do not have time for this. I do not have time for this. I do not have time for this. I do not have time for this. I do not have time for this. I do not have time for this. I do not have time for this. I do not have time for

this. I do not have time for this. I do not have time for this.

I

do

not h

ave time

for this. I do

not have time fo

r this. I do not have ti

me for this. I do not have ti

me for this. I do not have time for

this. I do not have time for this. I do not

have time for this. I do not have time for this.

I do not have time for this. I do not have time for this.

I do not have time for this. I do not have time for this. I do not have time for this. I do not have time for this. I do not have time for this. I do not have time for this. I do not have time for this. I do not have time for this. I do not have time for this. I do not have time for this. I do not have time for this. I do not have time for this. I do not have time for this. I do not have time for this. I do not have time for this. I do not have time for this. I do not have time for this. I do not have time for this. I do

not have time for this. I do not have time for this.

I do not have time for this. I do not have time for this. I do not have time for this. I do not have time for this. I do not have time for this. I do not have time for this. I do not have time for this. I do not have time for this. I do not have time for this. I do not have time for this. I do not have time for this. I do not have time for this. I do not have time for this. I do not have time for this. I do not have time for this. I do not have time for this. I do not have time for this. I do

not have time for this. I do not have time for this. I do not have time for this. I do not have time for this. I do not have time for this.

I do not

have time for

this. I do not have tim

e for this. I do not have time

for this. I do not have time for t

his. I do not have time for this. I

do not have time for this. I do n

ot have time for this. I do not

have time for this. I do not

have time for this. I do not

have time for this. I do not

have time for this. I do not

have time for this. I do not

have time for this. I do not

have time for this. I do not

have time for this. I do not

have time for this. I do not have time for this. I do not have time for this. I do not have time for this. I do not have time for this. I do not have time for this. I do not have time for this. I do

not have time for this. I do not have time for this. I do

not have time for this. I do not have time for this. I do

not have time for this. I do not have time for this. I do

not have time for this. I do not have time for this. I do

not have time for this. I do not have time for this. I do

not have time for this. I do not have time for this. I do

not have time for this. I do not have time for this. I do

not have time for this. I do not have time for this. I do

not have time for this. I do not have time for this. I do

not have time for this. I do not have time for this. I do

not have time for this. I do not have time for this. I do

not have time for this. I do not have time for this. I do

not have time for this. I do not have time for this. I do

not have time for this. I do not have time for this. I do

not have time for this. I do not have time for this. I do not have time for this. I do not have time for this. I do not have time for this. I do not have time for this.I do not have time for this. I do not have time for this.

I do not have time for this.

I do not have time for this. I do not have time for this. I do not have time for this. I do not have time for this. I do not have time for this. I do not have time for this. I do not have time for this. I do not have time for this. I do not have time for this. I do not have time for this. I do not have time for this. I do not have time for this. I do not have

time for this. I do not have time for this. I do not have time for this. I do not have time for this. I do not have time for this. I do not have time for this. I do not have time for this. I do not have time for this. I do not have time for this. I do not have time for this. I do not

have time for this. I do not

have time for this. I do not

have time for this. I do not

have time for this. I do not

have time for this. I do not

have time for this. I do not

have time for this. I do not

have time for this. I do not

have time for this. I do not

have time for this. I do not

have time for this. I do not

have time for this. I do not

have time for this. I do not

have time for this. I do not

have time for this. I do not

have time for this. I do not

have time for this. I do not have time for this. I do not have time for this. I do not have time for this. I do not have time for this. I do not have time for this. I do not have time for this. I do not have time for this. I do not have time for this. I do not have time for this. I do not have time for this. I do not have time for this. I do not have time for this. I do not have time for this. I do not have time for this. I do not have time for this.

I do not have time for this. I do not have time for this. I do not have time for this. I do not have time for this. I do not have time for this. I do not have time for this. I do not have time for this. I do not have time for this.

I do not have time for this. I do not have time for this. I do not have time for this.

I do not have time for this. I do not have time for this. I do not have time for this. I do not have time for this. I do not have time for this. I do not have time for this. I do not have time for this. I do not have time for this.

I do not have time for this. I do not have time for this. I do not have time for this. I do not have time for this. I do not have time for this. I do not have time for this.

I do not have time for this. I do not have time for this. I do

not have time for this.

I do not have time for this.

I do not have time for this.

I do

not have

time for

this.

I do not have time for this. I do not have time for this. I do not have time for this. I do not have time for this. I do not have time for this. I do not have time for this. I do not have time for this. I do not have time for this.

I do not have time for this. I do not have time for this. I do not have time for this. I do not have time for this. I do not have time for this. I do not have time for this. I do not have time for this. I do not have time for this. I do not have time for this. I do not have time for this.

I do not have time for this. I do not have time for this. I do not have time for this. I do not have time for this. I do not have time for this. I do not have time for this. I do not have time for this. I do not have time for this. I do not have time for this. I do not have time for this. I do not have time for this. I do not have time for this. I do not have time for this.

I do not have time for this.

I do not have time for this. I do not have time for this. I do not have time for this. I do not have time for this. I do not have time for this. I do not have time for this. I do not have time for this. I do not have time for this. I do not have time for this.

I do not have time for this. I do not have time for this. I do not have time for this. I do not have time for this. I do not have time for this.

I do not have time for this. I do not have

time for this. I do not have time for this. I do not have time for this. I do not have time for this. I do not have time for this. I do not have time for this. I do not have time for this. I do not have time for this. I do not have time for this. I do not have time for this. I do not have time for this. I do not have time for this. I do not have time for this. I do not have time for this. I do not have time for this. I do not have time for this. I do not have time for this.

I do not have time for this. I do not have time for this. I do not have time for this. I do not have time for this. I do not have time for this.

I do not have time for this. I do not have time for this. I do not have time for this. I do not have time for this. I do not have time for this. I do not have time for this.

I do not have time for this. I do not have time for this. I do not have time for this. I do not have time for this.

I do not have time for this. I do not have time for this. I do not have time for this. I do not have time for this.

I do not have time for this. I do not have time for this. I do not have time for this. I do not have time for this.

I do not have time for this. I do not have time for this. I do not have time for this. I do not have time for this.

I do not have time for this. I do not have time for this. I do not have time for this. I do not have time for this.

I do not have time for this. I do not have time for this. I do

not have time for this. I do not have time for this.

I do not have time for this. I do not have time for this. I do not have time for this. I do not have time for this. I do not have time for this.

I do not have time for this.

I do not have time for this. I do not have time for this.

I do not have time for this. I do not have time for this. I do not have time for this.

I do not have time for this. I do not have time for this. I do not have time for this. I do not have time for this.

I do not have time for this. I do not have time for this. I do not have time for this. I do not have time for this. I do not have time for this.

I do not have time for this. I do not have time for this. I do not have time for this. I do not have time for this. I do not have time for this. I do not have time for this.

I do not have time for this. I do not have time for this. I do not have time for this. I do not have time for this. I do not have time for this. I do not have time for this. I do not have time for this.

I do not have time for this. I do not have time for this.

I do not have time for this. I do not have time for this. I do

not have time for this. I do not have time for this.

I do not have time for this. I do not have time for this.

I do not have time for this.

I do not have time for this.

I do not have time for this.

I do not have time for this.

I do not have time for this.

I do not have time for this.

I do not have time for this.

I do not have time for this. I do not have time for this.

I do not have time for this. I do not have time for this. I do not have time for this. I do not have time for this.

I do not have time for this. I do not have time for this. I do not have time for this. I do not have time for this. I do not have time for this. I do not have time for this. I do not have time for this. I do not have time for this. I do not have time for this. I do

not have time for this. I do not have time for this.

I do not have time for this. I do not have

time for this. I do not have time for this.

I do not have time for this. I do not have time for this. I do not have time for this. I do not have time for this. I do not have time for this.

I do not have time for this. I do not have time for this. I do not have time for this. I do not have time for this.

I do not have time for this. I do not have time for this. I do not have time for this. I do not have time for this. I do not have time for this. I do not have time for this. I do not have time for this. I do not have time for this. I do not have time for this.

I do not have time for this. I do not have time for this. I do not have time for this. I do not have time for this. I do not have time for this. I do not have time for this. I do not have time for this. I do not have time for this. I do not have time for this. I do not have time for this. I do not have time for this. I do not have time for this. I do not have time for this.

I do not have time for this. I do not have time for this. I do not have time for this. I do not have time for this.

I do not have time for this. I do not have time for this. I do not have time for this. I do not have time for this. I do not have time for this. I do not have time for this. I do not have time for this. I do not have time for this. I do not have time for this. I do not have time for this. I do not have time for this. I do not have time for this. I do not have time for this. I do not have time for this. I do not have time for

this. I do not have time for this. I do not have time for this. I do not have time for this. I do not have time for this. I do not have time for this. I do not have time for this.

I

do not

have time for

this. I do not

have time for this. I

do not have time for this.

I do not have time for this.

I do not have time for this. I

do not have time for this. I do not

have time for this. I do not have time for

this. I do not have time for this. I do not

have time for this. I do not have time for this. I

do not have time for this. I do not have time for this.

I do not have time for this. I do not have time for this.

I do not have time for this. I do not have time for this. I

do not have time for this. I do not have time for this. I do not have time for this. I do not have time for this.

I do not have time for this. I do not have time for this. I do not have time for this. I do not have time for this. I do not have time for this. I do not have time for this. I do not have time for this. I do not have time for this. I do not have time for this. I do not have time for this. I do not have time for this. I do not have

time for this. I do not have time for this. I do not have time for this. I do not have time for this. I do not have time for this. I do not have time for this. I do not have time for this.

I do not have time for this. I do not have time for this. I do not have time for this. I do not have time for this. I do not have time for this. I do not have time for this. I do not have time for this. I do not have time for this. I

do not have time for this. I do not have time for this. I do not have time for this. I do not have time for this. I do not have time for this. I do not have time for this. I do not have

time for this. I do not have time for this. I do not have time for this. I do not have time for this. I do not

have time for this. I do not have time for this. I do not have time for this. I do not have time for this. I do not have time for this. I do not have time for this. I do not have time for this.

I do not have time for this. I do not have time for this. I

do not have time for this. I do not have time for this. I do not have time for this. I do not have time for this. I do not have time for this. I do not have time for this. I do not have time for this. I do not have time for this. I do not have time for this. I do not have time for this. I do not have time for this. I do not have time for this. I do not have time for this. I do not have time for this. I do not have time for this. I do not have time for this.

I do not have time for this. I do not have time for this. I do not have time for this. I do not have time for this. I do not have time for this. I do not have time for this. I do not have time for this. I do not have time for this. I do not have time for this. I do not have time for this. I do not have time for this. I do not have time for this. I do not have time for this. I do not have time for this. I do not have time for this. I do not have time for this. I do not have time for this. I do not have time for this.

I do not have time for this. I do not have time for this. I do not have time for this. I do not have time for this. I do not have time for this. I do not have time for this. I do not have time for this. I do not have time for this.

I do not have time for this. I do not have time for this. I do not have time for this. I do not have time for this. I do not have time for this.

I do not have time for this. I do not have time for this. I do not have time for this. I do not have time for this. I do not have time for this. I do not have time for this. I do not have time for this. I do not have time for this. I do not have time for this. I do not have time for this. I do not have time for this. I do not have time for this. I do not have time for this. I do not have

time for this. I do not have time for this. I do not have time for this. I do not have time for this. I do not have time for this. I do not have time for this. I do not have time for this. I do not have time for this. I do not have time for this. I do not have time for this. I do not have time for this. I

do not have time for this. I do not have time for this. I do not have time for this. I do not have time for this.

I do not have time for this. I do not have time for this. I do not have time for this. I do not have time for this. I do not have time for this. I do not have time for this. I do not have time for this. I do not have time for this. I do not have time for this. I do not have time for this. I do not have time for this. I do not have time for this. I do not have time for this. I do not have time for this. I do not have time for this. I do not have time for this.

I do not have time for this. I do not have time for this. I do not have time for this. I do not have time for this. I do not have time for this. I do not have time for this. I do not have time for this. I do not have time for this. I do not have time for this. I do not have time for this.

I do not have time for this. I do not have time for this. I do not have time for this.

I do not have time for this. I do not have time for this. I do not have time for this. I do not have time for this. I do not have time for this. I do not have time for this. I do not have time for this. I do not have time for this. I do not have time for this. I do not have time for this.

I do not have time for this. I do not have time for this.

I do not have time for this. I do not have time for this.

I do not have time for this. I do not have time for this.

I do not have time f

or this. I do not have ti

me for this. I do not have time for this. I do not have time for this. I do not have time for this. I do not have time for this. I

do not have time for this. I do not have time for this. I do not have time for this. I do not have time for this. I do not have time for this. I do not have time for this. I do no

t have time for this. I do not h

ave time for this. I d

o not have time for this. I do not have time for thi

s. I do not have time fo

r this. I do not have time for this. I do not have time for t

his. I do not have ti

me for this. I do not have time for this. I do not have time for this. I do not have time for this. I d

o not have time for this. I do not have ti

me for this. I do not have time for this. I do not have time

for this. I do not have time for th

is. I do not have time fo

r this. I do not have time for this. I do not have time for this. I do not have time for this.

I do not have time for this. I do n

ot have time for this. I do not have ti

me for this. I do not have time for this. I do not have time for this. I do not have time for this. I do not have

time for this. I do n

ot have time for this. I do not have time for this. I do not have time for this. I do not have time for t

his. I do not have t

ime for this. I do not have ti

me for this. I do not ha

ve time for this. I do not ha

ve time for this. I do not have time for this. I do not have time for this. I do not have time fo

r this. I do not have time for this. I do not have time for this. I do not have time for this. I do not have time for this. I do not have time for this. I do not have time for t

his. I do not have time for this. I d

o not have time for this. I do not have time for this. I do not have time for this. I do not have time f

or

this. I do not have time for this. I do not have time for this. I do not have time for this. I do not have time for this. I do not have time for this. I do not have time for this. I do not have time for this. I do not have time for this. I do not have time for this. I do not have time for this. I do not have time for this. I do not have time for this.

I do not have time for this.

I do not have time for this.

I do not have time for this.

I do not have time for this.

I do not have time for this.

I do not have time for this.

I do not have time for this.

I do not have time for this.

I do not have time for this.

I do not have time for this.

I do not have time for this.

I do not have time for this.

I do not have time for this.

I do not have time for this.

I do not have time for this.

I do not have time for this.

I do not have time for this.

I do not have time for this.

I do not have time for this.

I do not have time for this.

I do not have time for this.

I do not have time for this. I do

not have time for this. I do not have time for this. I do not have time for this. I do not have time for this. I do not have time for this. I do not have time for this.

I do not have time for this. I do not have time for this. I do not have time for this. I do not have time for this. I do not have time for this.

I do not have time for this. I do not have time for this. I do not have time for this. I do not have time for this. I do not have time for this. I do not have time for this. I do not have time for this. I do not have time for this. I do not have time for this.

I do not have time for this. I do not have time for this. I do not have time for this. I do not have time for this. I do not have time for this. I do not have time for this. I do not have time for this. I do not have time for this. I do not have time for this. I do not have time for this. I do not have time for this. I do not have time for this. I do not have time for this. I do not have time for this. I do not have time for this.

I do not have time for this. I do not have time for this. I do not have time for this. I do not have time for this. I do not have time for this. I do not have time for this.

I do not have time for this. I do not have time for this. I do not have time for this. I do not have time for this. I do not have time for this. I do not have time for this. I do not have time for this. I do not have time for this. I do not have time for this. I do not have time for this. I do not have time for this. I do not have time for this. I do not have time for this. I do not have time for

this. I do not have time for this. I do not have time for this. I do not have time for this. I do not have time for this. I do not have time for this. I do not have time for this. I do not have time for this. I do not have time for this. I do not have time for this. I do not have time for this. I do not have time for this. I do not have time for this. I do not have time for this. I do not have time for this.

I do not have time for this.

I do not have time for this. I do not have time for this. I do not have time for this. I do not have time for this. I do not have time for this. I do not have time for this. I do not have time for this. I do not have time for this. I do not have time for this. I do not have time for this. I do not have time for this. I do not have time for this.

I do not have time for this.

I do not have time for this. I do not have time for this.

I do not have time for this.

I do not have time for this. I do not have time for this.

I do

not have

time for

this.

I do not have time for this. I do not have time for this. I do not have time for this. I do not have time for this. I do not have time for this. I do not have time for this. I do not have time for this.

I do not have time for this. I do not have time for this. I do not have time for this. I do not have time for this. I do not have

time for this. I do not have time for this. I do not have time for this. I do not have time for this. I do not have time for this. I do not have time for this. I do not have time for this. I do not have time for this. I do not have time for this. I do not have time for this. I do not have time for this. I do not have time for this. I do not have time for this. I

do not have time for this. I do not have time for this.

I do not have time for this. I do not have time for this.

I do not have time for this.

I

do not

have time for

this. I do not

have time for this. I

do not have time for this.

I do not have time for this.

I do not have time for this. I

do not have time for this. I do not

have time for this. I do not have time for

this. I do not have time for this. I do not

have time for this. I do not have time for this. I

do not have time for this. I do not have time for this.

I do not have time for this. I do not have time for this.

I do not have time for this. I do not have time for this. I

do not have time for this. I do not have time for this. I do

not have time for this. I do not have time for this.

I do not have time for this. I do not have time for this.

I do not have time for this.

I do not have time for this. I do not have time for this.

I do not have time for this. I do not have time for this. I do not have time for this.

I do not have time for this. I do not have time for this. I do not have time for this. I do not have time for this.

I do not have time for this. I do not have time for this. I do not have time for this. I do not have time for this. I do not have time for this.

I do not have time for this. I do not have time for this. I do not have time for this. I do not have time for this. I do not have time for this. I do not have time for this.

I do not have time for this. I do not have time for this. I do not have time for this. I do not have time for this. I do not have time for this. I do not have time for this. I do not have time for this.

I do not have time for this. I do not have time for this.

I do not have time for this. I do

not have time for this. I do not have time for this.

I do not have time for this.

I do not have time for this. I do not have time for

this. I do not have time for this.

I do not have time for this.

I do not have time for this.

I do not have time for this. I do

not have time for this. I do not have time for this.

I do not have time for this.

I do not have time for this.

I do not have time for this.

I do not have time for this.

I do not have time for this. I do not have time for this. I do not have time for this. I do not have time for this. I do not have time for this. I do not have time for this. I do not have time for this. I do not have time for this. I do not have time for this. I do not have time for this. I do not have time for this. I do not have time for this. I do not have time for this. I do not have time for this. I do not have time for this. I do not have time for this. I do

not have time for this. I do not have time for this. I do not have time for this. I do not have time for this. I do not have time for this. I do not have time for this. I do not have time for this. I do not have time for this. I do not have time for this. I do not have time for this. I do not have time for this. I do not have time for this. I do not have time for this. I do not have time for this. I do not have time for this. I do not have time for this. I do not have time for this. I do not have time for this.

I do not have time for this.

I do not have time for this.

I do not have time for this.

I do not have time for this.

I do not have time for this.

I do not have time for this.

I do not have time for this.

I do not have time for this.

I do not have time for this. I do not have time for this. I do not have time for this. I do not have time for this. I do not have time for this. I do not have time for this. I do not have time for this. I do not have time for this. I do not have time for this. I do not have time for this. I do not have time for this. I do not have time for this. I do not have time for this. I do not have time for this. I do not have time for this. I do not have time for this. I do not have time for this. I do not have time for this. I do

not have time for this. I do not have time for this. I do not have time for this. I do not have time for this. I do not have time for this. I do not have time for this. I do not have time for this. I do not have time for this. I do not have time for this.

I do not have time for this.

I do not have time for this.

I do not have time for this.

I do not have time for this.

I do not have time for this.

I do not have time for this.

I do not have time for this.

I do not have time for this.

I do not have time for this.

I do not have time for this.

I do not have time for this.

I do not have time for this.

I do not have time for this.

I do not have time for this.

I do not have time for this.

I do not have time for this.

I do not have time for this. I do not have time for this. I do not have time for this. I do not have time for this. I do not have time for this. I do not have time for this. I do not have time for this. I do not have time for this. I do not have time for this. I do not have time for this. I do not have time for this. I do not have time for this. I do not have time for this. I do not have time for this. I

do not have time for this. I do not have time for this. I do not have time for this. I do not have time for this. I do not have time for this. I do not have time for this. I do not have

time for this. I do not have time for this. I do not have time for this. I do not have time for this. I do not

have time for this. I

do not have time for this. I do

not have time for this. I do not

have time for this. I do not have

time for this. I do not have time

for this. I do not have time for

this. I do not have time for this.

I do not have time for this. I do not have time for this. I do not have time for this. I do not have time for this. I do not have time for this. I do not have time for this. I do not have time for this. I do not have time for this. I do not have time for this. I do not have time for this.

I do not have time for this. I do not have time for this. I do not have time for this. I do not have time for this. I do not have time for this. I do not have time for this. I do not have time for this. I do not have time for this. I do not have time for this. I do not have time for this. I do not have time for this. I do not have time for this. I do not have time for this. I do not have time for this. I do not have time for this.

I do not have time for this.

I do not have time for

this. I do not have time

for this. I do not have

time for this. I do not

have time for this. I do

not have time for this. I

do not have time for this. I do not have time for this. I do not have time for this. I do not have time for this. I do not have time for this. I do not have time for this. I do not have time for this. I do not have time for this. I do not have time for this. I do

not have time for this. I do not have time for this. I do not have time for this. I do not have time for this.

I do not have time for this. I do not have time for this.

I do not have time for this. I do not have time for this. I do not have time for this.

I do not have time for this. I do not have time for this. I do not have time for this.

I do not have time for this. I do not have time for this. I do not have time for this.

I do not have time for this. I do not have time for this. I do not have time for this.

I do not have time for this. I do not have time for this. I do not have time for this.

I do not have time for this. I do not have time for this. I do not have time for this.

I do not have time for this. I do not have time for this. I do not have time for this.

I do not have time for this. I do not have time for this. I do not have time for this.

I do not have time for this. I do not have time for this. I do not have time for this.

I do not have time for this. I do not have time for this. I do not have time for this.

I do not have time for this. I do not have time for this. I do not have time for this. I do not have time for this. I do not have time for this. I do not have time for this. I do not have time for this. I do not have time for this. I do not have time for this. I do not have time for this. I do not have time for this.

I do not have time for this. I do not have time for this. I do not have time for this. I do not have time for this. I do not have time for this. I do not have time for this. I do not have time for this. I do not have time for this. I do not have time for this.

I do not have time for this. I do not have time for this. I do not have time for this. I do not have time for this. I do not have time for this. I do not have time for this.

I do not have time for this. I do not have time for this. I do not have time for this. I do not have time for this. I do not have time for this. I do not have time for this.

I do not have time for this. I do not have time for this. I do not have time for this. I do not have time for this. I do not have time for this. I do not have time for this.

I do not have time for this. I do not have time for this. I do not have time for this.

I do not have time for this.

I do not have time for this. I do not have time for this.

I do not have time for this.

I do not have time for this. I do not have time for this. I do not have time for this. I do not have time for this. I do not have time for this.

I do not have time for this.

I do not have time for this. I do not have time for this.

I do not have time for this.

I do not have time for this. I do not have time for this. I do not have time for this. I do not have time for this. I do not have time for this. I do not have time for this. I do not have time for this. I do not have time for

this. I do not have time for this. I do not have time for this. I do not have time for this. I do not have time for this. I do not have time for this. I do not have time for this. I do not have time for this. I do not have time for this.

I do not have time for this.

I do not have time for this. I do

not have time for this. I do not have

time for this. I do not have time for this.

I do not have time for this. I do not have

time for this. I do not have time for this.

I do not have time for this. I do not

have time for this. I do not

have time for this.

I do not

have time for this.

I do not have time for this.

I do not have time for this. I do not

have time for this. I do not have time for

this. I do not have time for this. I do not have time

for this. I do not have time for this. I do not have time for this. I do not have time for this. I do not have time for this. I do not have time for this. I do not have time for this. I do not have time for this. I do not have time for this. I do not have time for this. I do not have time for this. I do not have time for this. I do not have time for this. I do not have time for this. I do not have time for this. I do not have time for this. I do not have time for this.

I do not have time for this. I do

not have time for this. I do not have time for this. I do not have time for this. I do not have time for this. I do not have time for this. I

do not have time for this. I do not have time for this.

I

do not have time for this. I do not have time for this.

I

do not have time for this. I do not have time for this.

I

do not have time for this. I do not have time for this.

I

do not have time for this. I do not have time for this.

I

do not have time for this. I do not have time for this.

I

do not have time for this. I do not have time for this.

I

do not have time for this. I do not have time for this.

I

do not have time for this. I do not have time for this. I do not have time for this. I do not have time for this. I do not have time for this. I do not

have time for this. I do not have time for this.

I do not

have time for this. I do not have time for this.

I do not

have time for this. I do not have time for this.

I do not

have time for this. I do not have time for this.

I do not

have time for this. I do not have time for this.

I do not

have time for this. I do not have time for this.

I do not

have time for this. I do not have time for this.

I do not have time for this. I do not have time for this. I do

not have time for this. I do not have time for this.

I do not have time for this. I do not have time for this. I do not have time for this.

I do not have time for this. I do not have time for this. I do not have time for this. I do not have time for this. I do not have time for this. I do not have time for this.

I do not have time for this. I do not have time for this. I do not have time for this. I do not have time for this. I do not have time for this. I do not have time for this. I do not have time for this. I do not have time for this. I do not have time for this.

I do not have time for this. I do not have time for this. I do not have time for this. I do not have time for this. I do not have time for this. I do not have time for this. I do not have time for this. I do not have time for this. I do not have time for this.

I do not have time for this. I do not have time for this. I do not have time for this. I do not have time for this. I do not have time for this. I do not have time for this. I do not have time for this. I do not have time for this. I do not have time for this.

I do not have time for this. I do not have time for this. I do not have time for this.

I do not have time for this.

I do not have time for this. I do not have time for this.

I do not have time for this. I do not have time for this. I do not have time for this.

I do not have time for this. I do not have time for this. I do not have time for this. I do not have time for this.

I do not have time for this. I do not have time for this. I do not have time for this. I do not have time for this. I do not have time for this.

I do not have time for this. I do not have time for this. I do not have time for this. I do not have time for this. I do not have time for this. I do not have time for this.

I do not have time for this. I do not have time for this. I do not have time for this. I do not have time for this. I do not have time for this. I do not have time for this. I do not have time for this.

I do not have time for this. I do not have time for this. I do

not have time for this. I do not have time for this. I do not have time for this. I do not have time for this. I do not have time for this. I do not have time for this.

I do not have time for this. I do not have time for this. I do not have time for this. I do not have time for this. I do not have time for this. I do not have time for this. I do not have time for this. I do not have time for this. I do not have time for this.

I do not have time for this. I do not have time for this. I do not have time for this. I do not have time for this. I do not have time for this. I do not have time for this. I do not have time for this. I do not have time for this. I do not have time for this. I do not have time for this.

I do not have time for this. I do not have time for this.

I do

not have

time for

this.

I do not have time for this. I do not have time for this. I do not have time for this. I do not have time for this. I do not have time for this. I do not have time for this. I do not have time for this. I do not have time for this. I do not have time for this. I do not have time for this. I do not have time for this. I do not have time for this. I do not have time for this. I do not have time for this. I do not have time for this. I do not have time for this. I do

not have time for this. I do not have time for this. I do not have time for this. I do not have time for this. I do not have time for this. I

do not have time for this. I do

not have time for this. I do not

have time for this. I do not have

time for this. I do not have time

for this. I do not have time for

this. I do not have time for this.

I do not have time for this. I do not have time for

this. I do not have time for this. I do not have time

for this. I do not have time for this. I do not have

time for this. I do not have time for this. I do not

have time for this. I do not have time for this. I do

not have time for this. I do not have time for this. I

do not have time for this. I do not have time for this. I do

not have time for this. I do not have time for this. I do not

have time for this. I do not have time for this. I do not

have

time for this. I do not have time for this. I do not have time for this. I do not have time for this. I do not have time for

this. I do not have time for this. I do not have time for this.

I do not have time for this. I do not have time for this. I do not have time for this. I do not have time for this. I do not have time for this. I do not have time for this. I do not have time for this. I do not have time for this. I do not have time for th

is. I do not have time for this. I do not have tim

e for this. I do not have time for this. I do n

ot have time for this. I do not have time fo

r this. I do not have time for this. I do not hav

e time for this. I do not have time for this. I do no

t have time for this. I do not have time for this. I do no

t have time for this. I do not have time for this. I do not ha

ve time for this. I do not have time for this. I do not have time for this. I do not have time for this. I do not have time for this. I do not have time for this. I do not have time for this. I do not have time for this. I do not have time for this. I do not have time for this. I do not have time for this. I do not have time for

this. I do not have time for this. I do not have time for this. I do not have time for this. I do not have time for this. I do not have time for this. I do not have time for this. I do not have time for this. I do not have time for this. I do not have time for this. I do not have time for this. I do not have time for this. I do not have time for this. I do not have time for this.

I

do not have time for this.

I do not have time for this. I do not have

time for this. I do not have time for this. I do not have

time for this. I do not have time for this. I do not

have time for this. I do not have time

for this. I do not have time for

this. I do not have time for this.

I do not have time for this. I do not

have time for this. I do not have time for this.

I do not have time for this. I do not have time for this. I

do not have time for this. I do not have time for

this. I do not have time for this. I do

not have time for this. I do

not have time for

this. I do not have time for this. I do not have time for this. I do not have time for this. I do not have time for this. I do not

have time for this. I do not have time for this.

I do not have time for this. I do

not have

time

for

this.

I do not

have time for this. I do not have time

for this. I do not have time for this. I do not have

time for this. I do not have time for this. I do not have time for this. I do not have time for this. I do not have time for this.

I do not have time for this.

I do not have time for this.

I do not have time for this.

I do not have time for this. I do not have time for this. I do not have time for this. I do not have time for this. I do not have time for this. I do not have time for this. I do not have time for this. I do not have time for this. I do not have time for this. I do not have time for this. I do not have time for this. I do not have time for this.

I do not have time for this.

I do not have time for this. I do not have time for this.

I do not have time for this. I do not have time for this. I do not have time for this.

I do not have time for this. I do not have time for this. I do not have time for this. I do not have time for this.

I do not have time for this. I do not have time for this. I do not have time for this. I do not have time for this. I do not have time for this.

I do not have time for this. I do not have time for this. I do not have time for this. I do not have time for this. I do not have time for this. I do not have time for this.

I do not have time for this. I do not have time for this. I do not have time for this. I do not have time for this. I do not have time for this. I do not have time for this. I do not have time for this.

I do not have time for this.

I do not have time for this.

I do not have time for this. I do not have time for this. I do not have time for this. I do not have time for this. I do not have time for this. I do not have time for this. I do not have time for this. I do not have time for this.

I do not have

time

for this. I do not have

time

for this. I do not have

time

for this. I do not have

time

for this. I do not have

time

for this. I do not have

time

for this. I do not have

time

for this. I do not

have time for this. I do not have time for this. I do not have time for this. I do not have time for this. I do not have time for this. I do not have time for this.

I do not have time for this. I do not have time for this. I do not have time for this. I do not have time for this. I do not have time for this. I do not have time for this. I do not have time for this. I do not have time for this. I do not have time for this. I do not have time for this. I do not have time for this.

I do not have time for this. I do not have time for this. I do not have time for this. I do not have time for this. I do not have time for this. I do not have time for this. I do not have time for this. I do not have time for this. I do not have time for this. I do not have time for this. I do not have time for this. I do not have time for this. I do not have time for this.

I do not have time for this. I do not have time for this. I do not have time for this. I do not have time for this. I do not have time for this. I do not have time for this. I do not have time for this. I do not have time for this. I do not have time for this.

I do not have time for this.

I do not have time for this.

I do not have time for this.

I do not have time for this.

I do not have time for this.

I do not have time for this.

I do not have time for this.

I do not have time for this.

I do not have time for this.

I do not have time for this.

I do not have time for this.

I do not have time for this.

I do not have time for this.

I do not have time for this.

I do not have time for this.

I do not have time for this.

I do not have time for this.

I do not have time for this.

I do not have time for this.

I do not have time for this.

I do not have time for this.

I do not have time for this.

I do not have time for this.

I do not have time for this.

I do not have time for this.

I do not have time for this.

I do not have time for this.

I do not have time for this.

I do not have time for this.

I do not have time for this. I do not have time for this. I do not have time for this. I do not have time for this. I do not have time for this. I do not have time for this. I do not have time for this. I do not have time for this. I do not have time for this. I do not have time for this. I do not have time for this. I do not have time for this.

I do not have time for this. I do not have time for this. I do not have time for this. I do not have time for this.

I do not have time for this. I do not have time for this. I do not have time for this. I do not have time for this. I do not have time for this. I do not have time for this. I do not have time for

this. I do not have time for this.

I do not have time for this. I do

not have time for this. I do not have time for this. I do not have time for this. I do not have time for this.

I do not have time for this. I do not have time for this. I do not have time for this. I do not have time for this. I do not have time for this.

I do not have time for this. I do not have time for this. I do not have time for this. I do not have time for this. I do not have time for this. I do not have time for this. I do not have time for this. I do not have time for this. I do not have time for this. I do not have time for this. I do not have time for this. I do not have time for this. I do not have time for this.

I do not have time for this.

I do not have time for this. I do not have time for this. I do not have time for this. I do not have time for this. I do not have time for this. I do not have time for this. I do not have time for this. I do not have time for this. I do not have time for this. I do not have time for this.

I do not have time for this. I do not have time for this.

I do not have time for this.

I do not have time for this.

I do not have time for this. I do not have time for this.

I do not have time for this.

I do not have time for this. I do not have time for this. I do not have time for this. I do not have time for this. I do not have time for this. I do not have time for this. I do not have time for this. I do not have time for this. I do not have time for this. I do not have time for this. I do not have time for this. I do not have time for this. I do not have time for this.

I do not have time for this. I do not have time for this.

I do not have time for this. I do not have time for this.

I do not have time for this.

I do not have time for this.

I do not have time for this. I do not have time for this.

I do not have time for this. I do not have time for this.

I do not have time for this.

I do not have time for this. I do not have time for this.

I do not have time for this. I do not have time for this.

I do not have time for this.

I do not have time for this.

I do not have time for this. I do not have time for this.

I do not have time for this. I do not have time for this.

I do not have time for this.

I do not have time for this. I do not have time for this.

I do not have time for this. I do not have time for this.

I do not have time for this.

I do not have time for this.

I do not have time for this. I do not have time for this.

I do not have time for this.

I do not have time for this. I do not have time for this.

I do not have time for this. I do not have time for this.

I do not have time for this.

I do not have time for this.

I do not have time for this. I do not have time for this.

I do not have

time for th

is. I do not h

ave time for

this. I do n

ot have t

ime fo

r t

his. I do not have time for this. I do not have time for this. I do not have time for this. I do not have time for this. I do not have time for this.

I do not have time for this. I do not have time for this. I do not have time for this. I do not have time for this. I do not have time for this. I do not have time for this. I do not have time for this. I do not have time for this. I do not have time for this. I

do not have time for this. I do not have time for this. I do not have time for this. I do not have time for this. I do not have time for this. I do not have time for this. I do not have

time for this. I do not have time for this. I do not have time for this. I do not have time for this. I do not

have time for this. I do not have time for this. I do not have time for this. I do not have time for this. I do not have time for this. I do not have time for this. I do not have time for this.

I do not have time for this. I do not have time for this. I do not have time for this. I do not have time for this. I do not have time for this. I do not have time for this. I do not have time for this. I do not have time for this. I do not have time for this. I do not have time for this. I do not have time for this. I do not have time for this. I do not have time for this. I do not have

time for this. I do not have time for this. I do not have

time for this. I do not have time for this. I do not have time for this. I do not have time for this. I do not have time for this. I do not have time for this. I do not have time for this. I do not have time for this.

I do not have time for this. I do not have time for this.

I do not have time for this. I do not have time for this. I do not have time for this. I do not have time for this. I do not have

time for this. I do not have time for this.

I do not have time for this. I do not have time for

this. I do not have time for this.

I do not have time for this. I do

not have time for this. I do not have time for this. I do not have time for this. I do not have time for this. I do not have time for this. I do not have time for this. I do not have time for this. I do not have time for this. I do not have time for this. I do not have time for this. I do not have time for this. I do not have time for this. I do not have time for this. I do not have time for this. I do not have time for this. I do not have time for this. I do not have time for this.

I do not have time for this. I do not have time for

this. I do not have time for this.

I do

not have

time for

this.

I do not have time for this. I do not have time for this. I do not have time for this. I do not have time for this. I do not have time for this. I do not have time for this. I do not have time for this. I do not have time for this. I do not have time for this. I do not have time for this. I do not have time for this. I do not have time for this. I do not have time for this. I do not have time for this. I do not have time for this. I do not have time for this. I do not have time for this. I do not have time for this. I do not have time for this. I do not have

time for this. I do not have time for this.

I didn't ask for this.

I do not have time for this. I do not have time for

this. I do not have time for this.

I definitely do not have time for this.

I do not have time for this. I do not have

time for this. I do not have time for this. I do not have time for this. I do not have time for this. I do not have time for this. I do not have time for this. I do not have time for this.

I do not have time for this.

I do not have time for this. I do not have time for this.

I do not have time for this. I do not have time for this. I do not have time for this.

I do not have time for this. I do not have time for this. I do not have time for this. I do not have time for this.

I do not have time for this. I do not have time for this. I do not have time for this. I do not have time for this. I do not have time for this.

I do not have time for this. I do not have time for this. I do not have time for this. I do not have time for this. I do not have time for this. I do not have time for this.

I do not have time for this. I do not have time for this. I do not have time for this. I do not have time for this. I do not have time for this. I do not have time for this. I do not have time for this.

I do not have time for this. I do not have time for this.

I do not have time for this. I do not have time for this. I do not have time for this. I do not have time for this. I do not have time for this. I do not have time for this. I do not have time for

this. I do not have time for this.

I do not have time for this. I do not have time for this.

I do not have time for this.

I do not have time for this.

I do not have time for this.

I do not have time for this.

I do not have time for this.

I do not have time for this.

I do not have time for this.

I do not have time for this. I do not have time for this.

I do not have time for this. I do not have time for this. I do not have time for this. I do not have time for this.

I do not have time for this. I do not have time for this. I do not have time for this. I do not have time for this. I do not have time for this. I do not have time for this. I do not have time for this. I do not have time for this. I do not have time for this. I do not have time for this. I do not have time for this. I do not have time for this. I do not have time for this. I do not have time for this. I do not have time for this. I do not have time for

this. I do not have time for this.

I do not have time for this.

I do not have time for this. I do not have

time for this.

I do not have time for this. I do not have time for this. I do not have time for this. I do not have time for this. I do not have time for this.

I do not have time for this. I do not have time for this. I do not have time for this. I do not have time for this. I do not have time

for this. I do not have time for this.

I do not have time for this. I do not have time for this.

I do not have time for this. I do not have time for this. I do not have time for this. I do not have time for this. I do not have time for this. I do not have time for this. I do not have time

for this. I do not have time for this. I

do

not have time for this.

I do not have time for this. I do

not have time for this. I do not have time

for this. I do not have time for this. I do not have time

for this. I do not have time for this. I do not have time for this. I do not have time for this. I do not have time for this. I do not have time for this.

I do not have time for this. I do not have time for this. I do not have time for this. I do not have time for

this. I do not have time for

this. I do not have time for this. I do not have time for this. I do not have time for this. I do not have time for this. I do not have time for this. I do not have time for

this. I do not have time for this. I do not have time for

this. I do not have time for this. I do not have time for

this. I do not have time for this. I do not have time for

this. I do not have time for this. I do not have time for

this. I do not have time for this. I do not have time for

this. I do not have time for this. I do not have time for

this. I do not have time for this. I do not have time for

this. I do not have time for this. I do not have time for

this. I do not have time for this. I do not have time for

this. I do not have time for this. I do not have time for

this. I do not have time for this. I do not have time for

this. I do not have time for this. I do not have time for

this. I do not have time for this. I do not have time for

this. I do not have time for this. I do not have time for

this. I do not have time for this. I do not have time for

this. I do not have time for this. I do not have time for

this. I do not have time for this. I do not have time for this.

I do not have time for this. I do not have time for this. I do not have time for this. I do not have time for this. I do not have time for this. I do not have time for this. I do not have time for this. I do not have time for this. I do not have time for this. I do not have time for this. I do not have time for this. I do not have

time for this. I do not have time for this. I do not have time for this. I do not have time for this. I do not have time for this. I do not have time for this. I do not have time for this.

I do not have time for this. I do not have time for this. I do not have time for this. I do not have time for this. I do not have time for this. I do not have time for this. I do not have time for this. I do not have time for this. I

do not have time for this. I do not have time for this. I do not have time for this. I do not have time for this. I do not have time for this. I do not have time for this. I do not have

time for this. I do not have time for this. I do not have time for this. I do not have time for this. I do not

have time for this. I do not have time for this. I do not have time for this. I do not have time for this. I do not have time for this. I do not have time for this. I do not have time for this.

I do not have time for this. I do not have time for this. I do not have time for this. I do not have time for this. I do not have time for this. I do not have time for this. I do not have time for this. I do not have time for this. I do not have time for this. I do not have time for this. I do not have time for this. I do not have time for this. I do not have time for this. I do not have time for this.

I do not have time for this. I do not have time for this. I do not have time for this. I do not have time for this. I do not have time for this. I do not have time for this. I do not have time for this. I do not have time for this. I do not have time for this. I do not have time for this. I do not have time for this. I do not have time for this. I do not have time for this. I do not have time for this. I do not have time for this. I do not have time for this.

I do not have time for this. I do not have time for this.

I do not have time for this. I do not have time for this. I do not have time for this. I do not have time for this. I do not have time for this. I do not have time for this. I do not have time for this. I do not have time for this. I do not have time for this. I do not have time for this. I do not have time for this. I do not have time for this. I do not have time for this. I do not have time for this. I do not have time for this. I do not have time for this. I do not have time for this. I do not have time for this. I do not have

time for this. I do not have time for this. I do not have time for this. I do not have time for this. I do not have time for this. I do not have time for this. I do not have time for this. I do not have time for this. I do not have time for this. I do not have time for this. I do not have time for this. I do not have time for this. I do not have time for this. I do not have time for this. I do not have time for this. I do not have time for this. I do not have time for this. I do not have time for this. I do not have time for this. I do not

have time for this.

I do not have time for this. I do not

have time for this. I do not have time for this. I do

not have time for this. I do not have time for

this. I do not have time for this. I do not have time for this. I do not have time for this. I do not have time for this. I do not have time for this. I do not have time for this. I do not have time

for this. I do not have time for this.

I do not have time for

this. I do not have time for this. I do not have time

for this. I do not have time for this. I do not have time

for this. I do not have time for this. I do not have time

for this. I do not have time for this. I do not have time

for this. I do not have time for this. I do not have time

for this. I do not have time for this. I do not have time

for this. I do not have time for this. I do not have time

for this. I do not have time for this. I do not have time

for this. I do not have time for this. I do not have time

for this. I do not have time for this. I do not have time

for this. I do not have time for this. I do not have time

for this. I do not have time for this. I do not have time

for this. I do not have time for this. I do not have time

for this. I do not have time for this. I do not have time

for this. I do not have time for this. I do not have time

for this. I do not have time for this. I do not have time

for this. I do not have time for this. I do not have time

for this. I do not have time for this. I do not have time

for this. I do not have time for this. I do not have time for this.

I do not have time for this. I do not have time for this. I do not have time for this. I do not have time for this. I do not have time for this.

I do not have time for this. I do not have time for this. I do not have time for this. I do not have time for this. I do not have time for this.

I do not have time for this. I do not have time for this. I do not have time for this. I do not have time for this. I do not have time for this.

I do not have time for this. I do not have time for this. I do not have time for this. I do not have time for this. I do not have time for this.

I do not have time for this. I do not have time for this. I do not have time for this. I do not have time for this. I do not have time for this.

I do not have time for this. I do not have time for this. I do not have time for this. I do not have time for this. I do not have time for this.

I do not have time for this. I do not have time for this. I do not have time for this. I do not have time for this. I do not have time for this.

I do not have time for this. I do not have time for this. I do not have time for this. I do not have time for this. I do not have time for this.

I do not have time for this. I do not have time for this. I do not have time for this. I do not have time for this. I do not have time for this.

I do not have time for this. I do not have time for this. I do not have time for this. I do not have time for this. I do not have time for this.

I do not have time for this. I do not have time for this. I do not have time for this. I do not have time for this. I do not have time for this.

I do not have time for this. I do not have time for this. I do not have time for this. I do not have time for this. I do not have time for this.

I do not have time for this. I do not have time for this. I do not have time for this. I do not have time for this. I do not have time for this.

I do not have time for this. I do not have time for this. I do not have time for this. I do not have time for this. I do not have time for this.

I do not have time for this. I do not have time for this. I do not have time for this. I do not have time for this. I do not have time for this.

I do not have time for this. I do not have time for this. I do not have time for this. I do not have time for this. I do not have time for this. I do not have time for this. I do not have time for this. I do not have time for this. I do not have time for this. I do not have time for this. I do not have time for this. I do not have time for this. I do not have time for this. I do not have

time for this. I do not have time for this. I do not have

time for this. I do not have time for this. I do not have

time for this. I do not have time for this. I do not have

time for this. I do not have time for this. I do not have

time for this. I do not have time for this. I do not have

time for this. I do not have time for this. I do not have

time for this. I do not have time for this. I do not have

time for this. I do not have time for this. I do not have

time for this. I do not have time for this. I do not have time for this. I do not have time for this. I do not have time for this. I do not have time for this. I do not have time for this. I do not have time for this. I do not have time for this. I do not have time for this. I do not have time for this. I do not have time for this. I do not have time for this. I do not have time for this. I do not have time for this. I do not have time for this. I do not have

time for this. I do not have time for this. I do not have

time for this. I do not have time for this.

I do

not have

time for

this.

I do not have time for this. I do not have time

for this. I do not have

time for this. I do not have time for this.

I do not have time for this. I do not have time for this.

I do not have time for this. I do not have time for this.

I do not have time for this. I do not have time

for this. I do not have

time for this. I do not have time

for this. I do not have time for this. I do not have time

for this. I do not have time for this. I do not have time

for this. I do not have time

for this. I do not have

time for this.

I do not have time for this. I do not have time for this. I do not have time for this. I do not have time for this. I didn't ask for this. I do not have time for this. I do not have time for this. I do not have time for this. I do not have time for this. I do not have time for this. I do not have time for this. I do not have time for this. I do not have time for this. I do not have time for this. I do not have time for this. I do not have time for this. I do not have time for this. I do not have time for this. I do not have

time

for this. I do not have time for this. I do not have time

for

this. I do not have time for this. I do not have time for

this.

I do not have time for this. I do not have time for this.

I do

not have time for this. I do not have time for this. I do

not

have time for this. I do not have time for this. I do not

have

time

for this. I do not have time for this. I do not have time for this. I do not have time for this. I do not have time for this. I do not have time for this. I do not have time for this. I do not have time for this. I do not have time for this. I do not have time for this. I do not have time for this. I do not have time for this. I do not have time for this. I do not have time for this. I do not have time for this. I do not have time for this.

I do not have time for this. I do not have time for this. I do not hav

e time for this. I do not have time for this. I do not have time for this. I do not have time for thi

s. I do not have time for this. I do not have time for this. I do not have time for this. I do not have time for this. I do not have time for thi

s. I do not have time for this. I do not have time for this. I do not have time for this. I do no

t have time for this. I do not have time for this. I do not have time for this. I do n

ot have time for this. I do not have time for this. I do not have time for this. I do not have time f

or this. I do not have time for this. I do not have time for this. I do not have time fo

r this. I do not have time for this. I do not have time for this. I do not have time for this. I do not have ti

me for this. I do not have time for this. I do not have time for this. I do not have time for this. I d

o not have time for this. I do not have time for this. I do not have time for this. I do not have time for this. I do not have time for this. I didn't ask for this. I do not have time for this.

I do not have time for this.

I do not have time for this. I do not have time for this.

I do not have time for this. I do not have time for this. I do not have time for this.

I do not have time for this. I do not have time for this. I do not have time for this. I do not have time for this.

I do not have time for this. I do not have time for this. I do not have time for this. I do not have time for this. I do not have time for this.

I do not have time for this. I do not have time for this. I do not have time for this. I do not have time for this. I do not have time for this. I do not have time for this.

I do not have time for this. I do not

have time for this. I do not have time for this. I do not

have time for this. I do not have time for this. I do not

have time for this. I do not have time for this. I do not

have time for this. I do not have time for this. I do not

have time for this. I do not have time for this. I do not

have time for this. I do not have time for this. I do not

have time for this. I do not have time for this. I do not

have time for this. I do not have time for this. I do not

have time for this. I do not have time for this. I do not

have time for this. I do not have time for this. I do not

have time for this. I do not have time for this. I do not

have time for this. I do not have time for this. I do not

have time for this. I do not have time for this. I do not

have time for this. I do not have time for this. I do not

have time for this. I do not have time for this. I do not

have time for this. I do not have time for this. I do not

have time for this. I do not have time for this.

I do not have time for this.

I do not have time for this.

I do not have time for this.

I do not have time for this.

I do not have time for this.

I do not have time for this.

I do not have time for this.

I do not have time for this. I do not have time for this. I do not have time for this. I do not have time for this. I do not have time for this. I do not have time for this. I do not have time for this. I do not have time for this. I do not have time for this. I do not have time for this. I do not have time for this. I do not have time for this. I do not have time for this. I do not have time for this. I do not have time for this. I do not have time for this. I do not have time for this. I do not have time for this.

I do not have time for this.

I do not have time for this. I do not have time for this. I do not have time for this. I do not have time for this. I do not have time for this. I do not have time for this. I do not have time for this. I do not have time for this. I do not have time for this. I do not have time for this. I do not have time for this. I do not have time for this. I do not have time for this. I do not have time for this.

I do not have time for this. I do not have time for this. I do not have time for this. I do not have time for this.

I do not have time for this. I do

not have time for this. I do not have time for this. I do

not have time for this. I do not have time for this. I do

not have time for this. I do not have time for this. I do

not have time for this. I do not have time for this. I do

not have time for this. I do not have time for this. I do

not have time for this. I do not have time for this. I do

not have time for this. I do not have time for this. I do

not have time for this. I do not have time for this. I do

not have time for this. I do not have time for this. I do

not have time for this. I do not have time for this. I do

not have time for this. I do not have time for this. I do

not have time for this. I do not have time for this. I do

not have time for this. I do not have time for this. I do

not have time for this. I do not have time for this. I do

not have time for this. I do not have time for this. I do

not have time for this. I do not have time for this. I do

not have time for this. I do not have time for this. I do not have time for this. I do not have time for this. I do not have time for this. I do not have time for this. I do not have time for this. I do not have time for this. I do not have time for this. I do not have time for this. I do not have time for this. I do not have time for this. I do not have time for this. I do not hav

e time for this. I do not have time for this. I do not have time for this.

I do not have time for this. I do not have time for this. I do not have time for this. I do not have time for this. I do not have time for this.

I do not have time for this. I do not have time for this. I do not have time for this. I do not have time for this. I do not have time for this. I do not have time for this. I do not have time for this. I do not have time for this. I do not have time for this. I do

not have time for this. I do not have time for this. I do not have time for this. I do not have time for this. I do not have time for this. I do not have time for this. I do not have time for this. I do not have time for this. I do not have time for this. I do not have time for this.

I do not have time for this. I do not have time for this. I do not have time for this. I do not have time for this. I do not have time for this. I do not have time for this. I do not have time

for this. I do not have time for this. I do not have tim

e for this. I do not have time for this. I do not hav

e time for this. I do not have time for this. I d

o not have time for this. I do not have

time for this. I do not have time

for this. I do not have time

for this. I do not have

time for this. I do

not have t

ime for t

his. I do not

have time for t

his. I do not have tim

e for this. I do not have tim

e for this. I do not have time for thi

s. I do not have time for this. I do not have

time for this. I do not have time for this.

I do not have time for this. I do not have time for this. I do not have time for this. I do not have time for this. I do not have time for this. I do not have time for this. I do not have time for this. I do not have time for this. I do not have time for this. I do not have time for this. I do not have time for this. I do not have

time for this. I do not have time for this. I do not have time for this. I do not have time for this. I do not have time for this. I do not have time for this. I do not have time for this.

I do not have time for this. I do not have time for this. I do not have time for this. I do not have time for this. I do not have

time for this. I do not have time for this. I do not have time for this. I do not have time for this. I

do not have time for this. I do not have time for this. I do not have time for this. I do not have time for this. I do not have time for this. I do not have time for this. I do not have

time for this. I do not have time for this. I do not have time for this. I do not have time for this. I do not

have time for this. I do not have time for this. I do not have time for this. I do not have time for this. I

do not have time for this. I do not have time for this. I

do not have time for this. I do not have time for this. I

do not have time for this. I do not have time for this. I

do not have time for this. I do not have time for this. I

do not have time for this. I do not have time for this. I

do not have time for this. I do not have time for this. I

do not have time for this. I do not have time for this. I

do not have time for this. I do not have time for this. I

do not have time for this. I do not have time for this. I

do not have time for this. I do not have time for this. I

do not have time for this. I do not have time for this. I

do not have time for this. I do not have time for this. I

do not have time for this. I do not have time for this. I

do not have time for this. I do not have time for this. I

do not have time for this. I do not have time for this. I

do not have time for this. I do not have time for this. I

do not have time for this.

I do not have time for this. I do not have time for this.

I do not have time for this.

I do not have time for this. I do not have time for this.

I do not have time for this.

I do not have time for this. I

do not have time for this. I do not have time for this.

I do not have time for this. I do not

have time for this. I do not have time for this.

I do not have time for this. I do not have time

for this. I do not have time for this. I do not have time

for this. I do not have time for this.

I do not have time for this. I do not have time for this. I do not have time for this. I do not have time for this.

I do not have time for this. I

do not have time for this. I

do not have time for this. I do not have time for this. I do not have time for this. I do not have t

ime for this. I do not have time for this. I do not have time for this. I do not have time for this. I do not have time for this. I do not have time for this. I

do not have

time for this. I do not have time for this. I do not have time for this. I do not have time for th

is. I do not

have time for this. I do not have time for this. I do not have time for this. I do not have time for this. I do not have time for this. I do not have time f

or this. I do not have time for this. I do not have time for this. I do not have time for this. I do not ha

ve time for thi

s. I do not have time for this. I do not have time for this. I

do not have time for this. I do not have time for this. I do not have time for this. I do not have time for th

is. I do not h

ave time for this. I do not have tim

e for this. I do not have time for this. I do not have time for this. I do not have time for this. I do not have time for this. I do not have time for this. I do not have time for this. I do not have time for this. I do not have time for this. I do not have time for this. I do not have time for this. I do not have time for this. I do not have time for this.

I do not have time for this. I

do not have time for this. I do

not have time for this. I do not have

time for this. I do not have time

for this. I do not have time for

this. I do not have time for this.

I do not have time for this. I do not have time for this. I do not have time for this. I do not have time for this. I do not have time for this. I do not have time for this. I

do not have time for this. I do

not have time for this. I do not

have time for this. I do not have

time for this. I do not have time

for this. I do not have time for

this. I do not have time for this.

I do not have time for this. I do not have time for this. I do not have time for this. I do not have time for this. I do not have time for this. I do not have time for this. I do not have time for this. I do not have time for this. I do not have time for this. I do not have time for this.

I do not have time for this. I do not have time for this. I do not have time for this. I do not have time for this. I do not have time for this. I do not have time for this. I do not have time for this. I do not have time for this. I do not have time for this. I do not have time for this.

I do not have time for this. I do not have time for this. I do not have time for this. I do not have time for this. I do not have time for this. I do not have time for this. I do not have time for this. I do not have time for this. I do not have time for this. I do not have time for this.

I do not have time for this. I do not have time for this. I do not have time for this. I do not have time for this. I do not have time for this. I do not have time for this. I do not have time for this. I do not have time for this. I do not have time for this. I do not have time for this.

I do not have time for this. I do not have time for this. I do not have time for this. I do not have time for this. I do not have time for this. I do not have time for this. I do not have time for this. I do not have time for this. I do not have time for this. I do not have time for this.

I do not have time for this. I do not have time for this. I do not have time for this. I do not have time for this. I do not have time for this. I do not have time for this.

I do not have time for this.

I do not have time for this.

I do not have time for this.

I do not have time for this.

I do not have time for this.

I do not have time for this.

I do not have time for this.

I do not have time for this.

I do not have time for this.

I do not have time for this.

I do not have time for this.

I do not have time for this.

I do not have time for this.

I do not have time for this.

I do not have time for this.

I do not have time for this. I do

not have time for this. I do not have time for this.

I do not have time for this. I do not have time for this. I do not have time for this. I do not have time for this. I do not have time for this. I do not have time for this. I do not have time for this. I do not have time for this. I do not have time for this. I do not have time for this. I do not have time for this. I do not have time for this. I do not have time for this. I do not have time for this. I do not have time for this. I do not have time for this. I do not have time for this.

I do not have time for this. I do not have time for this. I do not have time for this. I do not have time for this. I do not have time for this. I do not have time for this. I do not have time for this. I do not have time for this. I do not have time for this. I do not have time for this. I do not have time for this. I do not have time for this. I do not have time for this. I do not have time for this. I do not have time for this. I do not have time for this. I do not have time for this. I do not have time for this.

I do not have time for this.

I do not have time for this. I do not have time for this. I do not have time for this. I do not have time for this. I do not have time for this. I do not have time for this. I do not have time for this. I do not have time for

this. I do not have time for this. I do not have time for this. I do not have time for this. I do not have time for this. I do not have time

for this. I do not have time for this. I do not have time for this. I do not have time for this. I do not have time for this. I do not have time for this. I do not have time for this. I do not have time for this. I do not have time for this. I do not have time for this. I do not have time for this. I do not have time for this. I do not have time for this. I do not have time for this. I do not have

time for this. I do not have time for this.

I do not have time for this. I do not have time for

this. I do not have time for this. I do not have time for this. I do not have time for this. I do not have time for this. I do not have time for this. I do not have time for this. I do not have time for this. I do not have time for this. I do not have time for this.

I do

not have

time for

this.

I do not have time for this. I do not have time for

this. I do not have time for this. I do not have time for this. I do not have time for this. I do not have time for this.

I do not have time for this. I do not have time for this. I do not have time for this. I do not have time for this. I do not have time for this. I do not have time for this. I do not have time for this. I do not have time for this. I do not have time for this.

I do not have time for this. I do not have time

for this. I do not have time for this. I do

not have time for this. I do not

have time for this. I

do not

have

time for this.

I do not have time

for this. I do not have time

for this. I do not have time for

this. I do not have time for this. I

do not have time for this. I do not have

time for this. I do not have time for this. I do

not have time for this. I do not have time for this.

I do not have time for this. I do not have time for this. I do not have time for this. I do not have time for this. I do not have time

for

this. I

do not have

time for this. I do

not have time for this.

I do not have time for this.

I do not have time for this. I do not have time

for this. I do not have time for this. I do not have time for this. I do not have time for this. I do not have time for this.

I do not have time for this. I do not have time

for this. I do not have time for this. I do not

have time for this. I do not have time

for this. I do not have time for

this. I do not have time

for this. I do not

have time

for this. I do not have time for this.

I do not have time for this. I do not have time for this.

I do not have time for this.

I do not have time for this. I do not have time for this.

I do not have time for this. I do not have time for this. I do not have time for this.

I do not have time for this. I do not have time for this. I do not have time for this. I do not have time for this.

I do not have time for this. I do not have time for this. I do not have time for this. I do not have time for this. I do not have time for this.

I do not have time for this. I do not have time for this. I do not have time for this. I do not have time for this. I do not have time for this. I do not have time for this.

I do not have time for this. I do not have time for this. I do not have time for this. I do not have time for this. I do not have time for this. I do not have time for this. I do not have time for this.

I do not have time for this. I do not have time for this.

I do not have time for this. I do not have time for this. I do not have time for this. I do not have time for this. I do not have time for this. I do not have time for this. I do not have time for this. I do not have time for this. I do not have time for this. I do not have time for this. I do not have time for this. I do not have time for this. I do not have time for this. I do not have time for this. I do not have time for this. I do not have time for this. I do not have time for this. I do

not have time for this. I do not have time for this. I do not have time for this. I do not have time for this. I do not have time for this. I do not have time for this. I do not have time for this. I do not have time for this. I do not have time for this. I do not have time for this. I do not have time for this. I do not have time for this. I do not have time for this. I do not have time for this. I do not have time for this. I do not have time for this. I do not have time for this. I do not have time for this.

I do not have time for this. I do not have time for this.

I do not have time for this.

I do not have time for this.

I do not have time for this.

I do not have time for this.

I do not have time for this.

I do not have time for this.

I do not have time for this.

I do not have time for this. I do not have time for this.

I do

not have

time for this. I do not have

time for this. I do not have time for this.

I do not have time for this. I do not have time for this. I do not have time for this. I do not have time for this. I do not

have time for this. I do not have time for

this. I do not have time for

this. I do not have time

for this. I

do

not have time for this. I do not have time for this.

I do not have time for this. I do not have

time for this. I do not have time for this. I do not have time for this. I do not have time for this. I do not have time for this. I do not

have time for this. I do not have time for this. I do not have time for

this. I do not have time for this. I do not have time for this. I do not

have time for this. I do not have time for this. I do not have time for this.

I do not have time for this. I do not have time for this. I do not have time for this.

I do not have time for this. I do not have time for this. I do not have time

for this. I do not have time for this. I do not have time for this.

I do not have time for this. I do not have time for this. I do not have time

for this. I do not have time for this. I do not have time for this. I do

not have time for this. I do not have time for this. I do not have

time for this. I do not have time for this. I do not have

time for this.

I do not have time for this. I do not have time for this. I do not have time for this. I do not have time for this. I do not have time for this. I do not have time for this. I do not have time for this. I do not have time for this. I do not have time for this. I do not have time for this. I do not have time for this. I do not have time for this. I do not have time for this. I do not have time for this. I do not have time for this. I do not have time for this. I do not have time for this.

I do not have time for this. I do not have time for this. I do not have time for this. I do not have time for this. I do not have time for this. I do not have time for this. I do not have time for this. I do not have time for this. I do not have time for this. I do not have time for this. I do not have time for this. I do not have time for this. I do not have time for this. I do not have time for this. I do not have time for this. I do not have time for this. I do not have time for this.

I do not have time for this. I do not have

time for this. I do not have time for this. I do not have time for this.

I do not have time for this. I do not have time for this. I do not have time for this. I do not have time for this. I do not have time for this. I do not have time for this. I do not have time for this. I do not have time for this. I do not have time for this. I do not have time for this. I do not have time for this. I do not have

time for this. I do not have time for this. I do not have time for this. I do not have time for this. I do not have time for this. I do not have time for this. I do not have time for this.

I do not have time for this. I do not have time for this. I do not have time for this. I do not have time for this. I do not have time for this. I do not have time for this. I do not have time for this. I do not have time for this. I

do not have time for this. I do not have time for this. I do not have time for this. I do not have time for this. I do not have time for this. I do not have time for this. I do not have

time for this. I do not have time for this. I do not have time for this. I do not have time for this. I do not

have time for this. I do not have time for this. I do not have time for this. I do not have time for this. I do not have time for this. I do not have time for this. I do not have time for this.

I do not have time for this. I do not have time for this. I

do not have time for this. I do not have time for this. I do not have time for this. I do not have time for this. I do not have time for this.

I do not

have time for

this. I do not have

time for this. I do not have

time for this. I do not have time

for this. I do not have time for this. I do

not have time for this. I do not have time for this.

I do not have time for this. I do not have time for this. I do not have time for this. I do not have time for this. I do not have time for this. I do not have time for this. I do not have time

for this. I do not have time for this. I do not have

time for this. I do not have time for this. I do

not have time for this. I do not have time

for this. I do not have time for this.

I do not have time for this.

I do not have time for

this. I do not have

time

for this.

I do not have

time for this. I do

not have time for this.

I do not have time for this.

I do not have time for this. I do

not have time for this. I do not have

time for this. I do not have time for this.

I do not have time for this. I do not have time

for this. I do not have time for this. I do not have

time for this. I do not have time for this. I do not have

time for this. I do not have time for this. I do not have time for this. I do not have time for this. I do not have time for this. I do not have time for this. I do not have time for this. I do not have time for this. I do not have time for this. I do not have

time for this. I do not have time for this. I do not have

time for this. I do not have time for this. I do not

have time for this. I do not have time for this.

I do not have time for this. I do not have time

for this. I do not have time for this. I do not

have time for this. I do not have time for

this. I do not have time for this. I do not

have time for this. I do not have time

for this. I do not have time for this. I

do not have time for this. I do not

have time for this. I do not have

time for this. I do not have time

for this. I do not have time for

this. I do not have time for

this. I do not have time

for this. I do not have

time for this. I do not

have time for this. I

do not have time

for this. I do

not have

time for

this. I

do

not have

time for this.

I do not have time

for this. I do not have time

for this. I do not have time for this.

I do not have time for this. I do not have

time for this. I do not have time for this. I do not

have time for this. I do not have time for this. I do not

have time for this. I do not have time for this.

I do not have time for this. I do not have

time for this. I do not have time for this.

I do not have time for this. I do not have time for this. I do not have time for this. I do not have time for this. I do not have time for this. I do not have time for this.

I do not have time for this. I do not have time for this. I do not have time for this. I do not have time for this. I do not have time for this. I do not have time for this. I do not have time for this. I do not have time for this. I do not have time for this. I do not have time for this. I do not have time for this. I do not have time for this. I do not have time for this. I do not have time for this. I do not have time for this.

I

do not have time for this. I do not have time for this. I do not have time for this. I do not have time for this. I do not have time for this. I do not have time for this. I do not have time for this. I do not have time for this. I do not have time for this. I do not have time for this. I do not have time for this. I do not have time for this. I do not have time for this.

I do not have time for this. I do not have time for this. I do not have time for this. I do not have time for this. I do not have time for this. I do not have time for this. I do not have time for this. I do not have time for this. I do not have time for this. I do not have time for this. I do not have time for this. I do not have time for this.

I do not have time for this. I do not have time for this. I do not have time for this.

I do not have time for this. I do not have time for this. I do

not have time for this.

I do not have time for this. I do not have time for this. I do not have time for this.

I do not have time for this. I do not have time for this. I do not have time for this.

I do not have time for this. I do not have time for this. I do not have time for this.

I do not have time for this. I do not have time for this. I do not have time for this.

I do not have time for this. I do not have time for this. I do not have time for this.

I do not have time for this. I do not have time for this. I do not have time for this.

I do not have time for this. I do not have time for this. I do not have time for this.

I do not have time for this. I do not have time for this. I do not have time for this.

I do not have time for this. I do not have time for this. I do not have time for this.

I do not have time for this. I do not have time for this. I do not have time for this.

I do not have time for this. I do not have time for this. I do not have time for this. I do not have time for this. I do not have time for this. I do not have time for this. I do not have time for this. I do not have time for this. I do not have time for this. I do not have time for this. I do not have time for this. I do not have time for this. I do not have time for this. I do not have time for this. I do not have time for this. I do not have time for this. I do not have time for

this.

I

do not have time for this. I do not have time for this. I do not have time for this. I do not have time for this. I do not have time for this. I do not have time for this. I do not have time for this. I do not have time for this. I do not have time for this. I do not have time for this. I do

not

have time for this. I do not have time for this. I do not have time for this. I do not have time for this. I do not have time for this.

I

do

not

have time for this.

I do not have time for this. I do not have time for this. I do not have time for this.

I do not have time for this. I do not have time for this. I do not have time for this.

I do not have time for this. I do not have time for this. I do not have time for this.

I do not have time for this.

I do not have time for this. I do not have time for this. I do not have time for this.

I do not have time for this. I do not have time for this. I do not have time for this. I do not have time for this. I do not have time for this. I do not have time for this. I do not have time for this. I do not have time for this.

I do not have time for this. I do not have time for this. I do not have time for this. I do not have time for this. I do not have time for this. I do not have time for this.

I do not have time for this. I do not have time for this. I do not have time for this. I do not have time for this. I do not have time for this. I do not have time for this. I do not have time for this. I do not have time for this.

I do not have time for this. I do not have time for this. I do not have time for this.

I do not have time for this. I do not have time for this. I do

not have time for this. I do not have time for this. I do not have time for this. I do not have time for this. I do not have time for this. I do not have time for this. I do not have time for this. I do not have time for this. I do not have time for this. I do not have time for this. I do not have time for this.

I

do not have time for this. I do not have time for this. I do not have time for this.

I

do not have time for this. I do not have time for this. I do not have time for this. I do not have time for this. I do not have time for this. I do not have time for this.

I

do not have time for this. I do not have time for this. I do not have time for this. I do not have time for this. I do not have time for this. I do not have time for this. I do not have time for this. I do not have time for this.

I

do not have time for this. I do not have time for this. I do not have time for this. I do not have time for this. I do not have time for this. I do not have time for this. I do not have time for this. I do not have time for this. I do not have time for this. I do not have time for this. I do not have time for this. I do not have time for this. I do not have time for this. I do not have time for this. I do not have time for

this. I do not have time for this. I

do

not have time for this. I do not have time for this. I do not have time for this. I

do

not have time for this. I do not have time for this. I do not have time for this. I do not have time for this. I do not have time for this. I

do

not have time for this. I do not have time for this. I do not have time for this. I do not have time for this. I do not have time for this. I do not have time for this. I do not have time for this. I do not have time for this. I do not have time for this. I do not have time for this. I do not have time for this. I do not have time for this. I

do

not have time for this. I do not have time for this. I do not have time for this. I do not have time for this. I do not have time for this. I do not have time for this. I do not have time for this. I do not have time for this. I do not have time for this. I do not have time for this. I do not have time for this. I do not have time for this. I do not have time for this. I do not have time for this. I do not have time for this. I do not have time for this. I do not have time for this. I do not have time for this. I do not have

time for this. I do

not

have time for this. I do not have time for this. I do not have time for this. I do not have time for this. I do not have time for this. I do not have time for this. I do not have time for this. I do not have time for this. I do not have time for this. I do not have time for this. I do

not

have time for this. I do not have time for this. I do not have time for this. I do not have time for this. I do not have time for this. I do not have time for this. I do not have time for this. I do not have time for this. I do not have time for this. I do not have time for this. I do not have time for this. I do

not

have time for this. I do not have time for this. I do not have time for this. I do not have time for this. I do not have time for this. I do not have time for this. I do not have time for this. I do not have time for this. I do

not

have time for this. I do not have time for this. I do not have time for this. I do not have time for this. I do not have time for this. I do not have time for this. I do not have time for this. I do not have time for this. I do not have time for this. I do not have time for this. I do not have time for this. I do not have

time for this. I do not have time for this. I do not have time for this. I do not have time for this. I do not have time for this. I do not have time for this. I do not have time for this. I do not

have

time for this. I do not have time for this. I do not have time for this. I do not have time for this. I do not have time for this. I do not have time for this. I do not

have

time for this. I do not have time for this. I do not have time for this. I do not have time for this. I do not have time for this. I do not have time for this. I do not have time for this. I do not have time for this. I do not have time for this. I do not have time for this. I do not have time for this. I do not have time for this. I do not have time for this. I do not have time for this. I do not have time for this. I do not

have

time for this. I do not have time for this. I do not have time for this. I do not have time for this. I do not have time for this. I do not have time for this. I do not

have

time for this. I do not have time for this. I do not have time for this. I do not have time for this. I do not have time for this. I do not have time for this. I do not have time for this. I do not have time for this. I do not have time for this. I do not have

time for this. I do not have time for this. I do not have time for this. I do not have time for this. I do not have time for this. I do not have time for this. I do not have time for this. I do not have time for this. I do not have

time

for this. I do not have time for this. I do not have time for this. I do not have time for this. I do not have time for this. I do not have

time

for this. I do not have time for this. I do not have time for this. I do not have

time

for this. I do not have time for this. I do not have time for this. I do not have

time

for this. I do not have time for this. I do not have time for this. I do not have time for this. I do not have time for this. I do not have time for this. I do not have time for this. I do not have time for this. I do not have time for this. I do not have time for this. I do not have time for this. I do not have time for this. I do not have time for this. I do not have time for this. I do not have time for this. I do not have time for this. I do not have time for this. I do not have time for this. I do not have time for this. I do not have time for this. I do not have

time for this. I do not have time for this. I do not have time for this. I do not have time for this. I do not have time for this. I do not have time for this. I do not have time for this. I do not have time for this. I do not have time

for

this. I do not have time for this. I do not have time for this. I do not have time for this. I do not have time for this. I do not have time for this. I do not have time

for

this. I do not have time for this. I do not have time for this. I do not have time for this. I do not have time for this. I do not have time for this. I do not have time

for

this. I do not have time for this. I do not have time for this. I do not have time for this. I do not have time for this. I do not have time

for

this. I do not have time for this. I do not have time for this. I do not have time for this. I do not have time for this. I do not have time for this. I do not have time for this. I do not have time for this. I do not have time for this. I do not have time for this. I do not have time for this. I do not have time for this. I do not have time for this. I do not have time for this. I do not have time for this. I do not have time for

this. I do not have time for this. I do not have time for this. I do not have time for this. I do not have time for this. I do not have time for this. I do not have time for this. I do not have time for this. I do not have time for this. I do not have time for

this.

I do not have time for this. I do not have time for this. I do not have time for this. I do not have time for this. I do not have time for this. I do not have time for

this.

I do not have time for this. I do not have time for this. I do not have time for this. I do not have time for this. I do not have time for this. I do not have time for

this.

I do not have time for this. I do not have time for this. I do not have time for this. I do not have time for this. I do not have time for this. I do not have time for

this.

I do not have time for this. I do not have time for this. I do not have time for this. I do not have time for this. I do not have time for this. I do not have time for this. I do not have time for this. I do not have time for this. I do not have time for this. I do not have time for this. I do not have time for this. I do not have time for this. I do not have time for this. I do not have time for this. I do not have time for this. I do not have time for this. I do

not have time for this. I do not have time for this. I do not have time for this. I do not have time for this.

I do not have time for this.

I definitely do not have time for this.

I do not have time for this. I do not have time for this.

I do not have time for this. I do not have time for this. I do not have time for this.

I do not have time for this. I do not have time for this. I do not have time for this. I do not have time for this.

I do not have time for this. I do not have time for this. I do not have time for this. I do not have time for this. I do not have time for this.

I do not have time for this. I do not have time for this. I do not have time for this. I do not have time for this. I do not have time for this. I do not have time for this.

I do not have time for this. I do not have time for this. I do not have time for this. I do not have time for this. I do not have time for this. I do not have time for this. I do not have time for this.

I do not have time for this. I do not have time for this.

I do not have time for this. I do not have time for this.

I do not have time for this. I do not have time for this.

I do not have time for this.

I do not have time for this.

I do not have time for this.

I do not have time for this.

I do not have time for this.

I do not have time for this.

I do not have time for this.

I do not have time for this. I do not have time for this.

I do not have time for this. I do not have time for this. I do not have time for this. I do not have time for this.

I do not have time for this. I do not have time for this. I do not have time for this. I do not have time for this. I do not have time for this. I do not have time for this. I do not have time for this. I do not have time for this. I do not have time for this. I do

not have time for this. I do not have time for this.

We do not have time for this.

We do not have time for this.

We do not have time for this.

We do not have time for this.

We do not have time for this.

I do not have time for this. I do not have time for this. I do not have time for this. I do not have time for this. I do not have

time for this. I do not have time for this. I do not have time for this. I do not have time for this. I do not have time for this. I do not have time for this. I do not have time for this. I do not have time for this. I d

o not have time for

this. I do not have time for t

his. I do not have time for this. I do not have time for this. I do not have time for this. I do not have ti

me for this. I

do not have time

for this. I do not have time for this. I do

not have time for this. I do not have time for this. I do not have time for this. I do not have time for this. I do not have time for this. I do not

have time for this. I do not have ti

me for this. I do not have time for this. I do not have time for this

. I do not have ti

me for this. I do not have time for t

his. I do not have time for this. I do not have time for this. I do not have time for this.

I do not have time for this. I do not have time for this. I do not have time for this. I do not have time for this. I do not have time for this.

I do not have time for this. I do not have time for this.

I do not have time for this. I do

not have time for this.

I

D

o

N

o

t

H

a

v

e

T

i

m

e

F

o

r

T

h

i

s

.

I do not have time for this. I do not have time for this. I do not have time for this. I do not have time for this. I do not have time for this. I do not have time for this. I do not have time for this. I do not have time for this. I do not have time for this. I do not have time for this. I do not have time for this. I do not have time for this.

I do not have time for this. I do not have time for this. I do not have time for this. I do not have time for this. I do not have time for this. I do not have time for this. I do not have time for this. I do not have time for this. I do not have time for this. I do not have time for this. I do not have time for this. I do not have

time for this. I do not have time for this. I do not have time for this. I do not have time for this. I do not have time for this. I do not have time for this. I do not have time for this.

I do not have time for this. I do not have time for this. I do not have time for this. I do not have time for this. I do not have time for this. I do not have time for this. I do not have time for

this. I do not have time for this. I

do not have time for this. I do not have time for this. I do not have time for this. I do not have time for this. I do not have time for this. I do not have time for this. I do not have

time for this. I do not

have time for this. I do not have time for this. I do not have time for this. I do not

have time

for this. I do not have time for this. I do not have time for this. I do not have time for this. I do not have time for this. I do not have time for this. I do not have time

for this.

I do not have time for this. I do not have

time for this. I do not have time for this. I do not have time for this. I do not have time for this. I do not have time for this. I do not have time for this. I do not have time for this.

I do not have time for this. I do not have time for this.

I do not have time for this. I do not have time for this. I do not have time for this. I do not have time for this. I do not have time for this. I do not have time for this. I do not have time for this. I do not have time for this. I do not have time for this. I do not have time for this. I do not have time for this. I do not have time for this. I do not have time for this. I do not have time for this. I do not have time for

this. I do not have time for this.

I do not have time for this. I do not have time for this. I do not have time for this. I do not have time for this. I do not have time for this. I do not have time for this. I do not have time for this. I do not have time for this. I do not have time for this.

I do not have time for this. I do not have

time for this. I do not have time for this. I do not have time for this. I do not have time for this. I do not have time for this. I do not have time for this. I do not have time for this. I do not have time for this. I do not have time for this. I do not have time for this. I do not have time for this. I do not have time for this. I do not have time for this. I do not have time for this.

I do not have time for this. I do not have time for this.

I do not have time for this. I do not have time for this. I do not have time for this. I do not have time for this. I do not have time for this. I do not have time for this. I do not have time for this. I do not have time for this. I do not have time for this. I do not have time for this. I do not have time for this. I do not have time for this.

I do not have time for this. I do not have time for this. I do not have time for this. I do not have time for this. I do not have time for this. I do not have time for this. I do not have time for this. I do not have time for this. I do not have time for this. I do not have time for this. I do not have time for this. I do not have time for this. I do not have time for this. I do not have time for this. I do not have time for this. I do not have time for this. I do not have time for this. I do

not have time for this.

I do not

have time for

this. I do not

have time for

this. I do not have

time for this. I do

not have time for this. I do not have time for this.

I do not have time for this.

I do not have time for this. I do

not have time for this. I do not have

time for this. I do not have time for this. I do

not have time for this. I do not have time for this. I do not have time for this. I do not have time for this. I do not have time for this.

I do not have time for this. I do not have time for this.

I do not have time for this. I do not have time for this.

I do not have time for this. I do not have time for this.

I do not have time for this. I do not have time for this.

I do not have time for this. I do not have time for this.

I do not have time for this. I do not have time for this.

I do not have time for this. I do not have time for this.

I do not have time for this. I do not have time for this.

I do not have time for this. I do not have time for this.

I do not have time for this. I do not have time for this.

I do not have time for this. I do not have time for this.

I do not have time for this. I do not have time for this.

I do not have time for this. I do not have time for this.

I do not have time for this. I do not have time for this.

I do not have time for this. I do not have time for this.

I do not have time for this. I do not have time for this.

I do not have time for this. I do not have time for this.

I do not have time for this. I do not have time for this.

I do not have time for this. I do not have time for this.

I do not have time for this. I do not have time for this.

I do not have time for this. I do not have time for this. I do not have time for t

his. I do not h

ave time f

or this. I do not have time fo

r this. I do n

ot have time

for this. I do n

ot have time fo

r this. I do not hav

e time for this. I do n

ot have time for t

his. I do not have ti

me for this. I do not h

ave time for this. I d

o not have time for this. I

do

not have time for this. I do not have time for this. I do not have time for this. I do not have time for this. I do not

have time for this. I do not have time for this.

I do not have time for this. I do not have time for this. I do not have time for this. I do not have time for this. I do not have

time for this. I do not have time for this.

I do

not have

time for

this.

I do not have time for this. I do not have

time for this. I do not have

time for this. I do not have

time for this. I do not have

time for this. I do not have

time for this. I do not have

time for this. I do not have

time for this. I do not have

time for this. I do not have

time for this. I do not have

time for this. I do not have

time for this. I do not have

time for this. I do not have

time for this. I do not have

time for this. I do not have

time for this. I do not have

time for this. I do not have

time for this. I do not have

time for this. I do not have time for this. I do not have time for this. I do not have time for this.

I

do not

have time for this.

I do not have time for this. I do not have

time for this. I do not have time for this. I do not have time for this. I do not have time for this. I do not have time for this. I do not have time for this. I do not have time for this.

I do not have time

for this.

I

do not have time for this. I do not have

time for

this.

I do not

have time for

this. I do not have

time for this. I do not

have time for this. I do

not have time for this. I do

not have time for this. I do

not have time for this. I

do not have time for

this. I do not have

time for this. I do

not have time

for this. I do

not have

time

for this. I do not have time for this.

I do not have time for this. I do not have

time for this. I do not have time for this. I do

not have time for this. I do not have time for this.

I do not have time for this. I do not have time for this.

I do not have time for this. I do not have time for this. I

do not have time for this. I do not have time for this. I do not have time for this. I do not have time for this. I do not have time for this. I do not have time for this. I do not have time for this.

I do not have time for this. I do not have time for this. I

do not have time for this. I do not have time for this. I

do not have time for this. I do not have time for this. I

do not have time for this. I do not have time for this.

I do not have time for this. I do not have time for

this. I do not have time for this. I do not have

time for this. I do not have time for

this. I do not have time for

this. I didn't ask for

this. I do not have time for this.

I do not have time for this.

I do not have time for this. I do not have time for this.

I do not have time for this. I do not have time for this. I do not have time for this.

I do not have time for this. I do not have time for this. I do not have time for this. I do not have time for this.

I do not have time for this. I do not have time for this. I do not have time for this. I do not have time for this. I do not have time for this.

I do not have time for this. I do not have time for this. I do not have time for this. I do not have time for this. I do not have time for this. I do not have time for this.

I do not have time for this. I do not have time for this. I do not have time for this. I do not have time for this. I do not have time for this. I do not have time for this. I do not have time for this.

I do not have time for this. I do not have time for this. I do not have time for this.

I do not have time for this. I do not have time for this. I do not have time for this. I do not have time for this. I do not have time for this. I do not have time for this. I do not have time for this. I do not have time for this. I do not have time for this. I do not have time for this. I do not have time for this. I do not have time for this.

I do not have time for this. I do not have time for this.

I do not have time for this. I do not have time for this. I do not have time for this. I do not have time for this. I do not have time for this. I do not have time for this. I do not have time for this. I do not have time for this. I do not have time for this. I do not have time for this. I do not have time for this. I do not have time for this. I do not have time for this. I do not have time for this. I do not have time for this.

I do not have time for this.

I do not have time for this. I do not have time for this. I do not have time for this. I do not have time for this. I do not have time for this. I do not have time for this. I do not have time for this. I do not have time for this. I do not have time for this. I do

not have time for this. I do not have time for this. I do not have time for this. I do not have time for this. I do not have time for this. I do not have time for this. I do not have time for this. I do not have time for this. I do not have time for this. I do not have time for this. I do not have time for this. I do not have time for this.

I do not have time for this.

I do not have time for this.

I do not have time for this.

I do not have time for this.

I do not have time for this.

I do not have time for this.

I do not have time for this.

I do not have time for this.

I do not have time for this.

I do not have time for this.

I do not have time for this.

I do not have time for this.

I do not have time for this.

I do not have time for this. I do not have time for this. I do

not have time for this. I do not have time for this. I do not have time for this. I do not have time for this. I do not have time for this. I do not have time for this. I do not have time for this. I do not have time for this.

I do not have time for this. I do not have time for this. I do not have time for this. I do not have time for this.

I do not have time for this.

I do not have time for this. I do not have time for this. I do not have time for this. I do not have time for this. I do not have time for this. I do not have time for this. I do not have time for this. I do not have time for this. I do not have time for this. I do not have time for this. I do not have time for this. I do not have time for this. I do not have time for this. I do not have time for this. I do not have time for this.

I do not have time for this. I do not have time for this. I do not have time for this. I do not have time for this.

I do not have time for this.

I do not have time for this. I do not have time for this. I do not have time for this. I do not have time for this. I do not have time for this. I do not have time for this. I do not have time for this. I do not have time for this. I do not have time for this. I do not have time for this. I do not have time for this. I do not have time for this.

I do not have time for this. I do not have time for this. I do

not have time for this. I do not have time for this. I do not have time for this. I do not have time

for this. I do not have time

for this. I do not have time for this. I do not have time

for this. I do not have time for this.

I do not have

time

for this. I do not have

time for this. I do not have time for this.

I do not have time for this. I do not have time for this. I

do not have time for this. I do not

have

time for this. I do not have

time for this. I do not have time for this. I do not have

time for this. I do not have

time

for this. I do not have time for this.

I do not have time for this. I do not have time for this. I do not have time for this. I do not have time for this. I do not have time for this. I do not have time for this. I do not have time for this. I do not have time for this. I do not have time for

this.

I do not have

time for this.

I do not have

time for this.

I do not have

time for this.

I do not have

time for this.

I do not have

time for this.

I do not have

time for this. I do not have time for this. I do not have time for this. I do not have time for this. I do not have time for this. I do not have time for this. I do not have time for this. I do not have time for this. I do not have time for this. I do not have

time for this. I do not have time for t

his. I do not h

ave time for t

his. I do not h

ave time for t

his. I do not h

ave time for t

his. I do not h

ave time for t

his.

I do not have time for this. I do not have time for this. I do not have time for this. I do not have time for this. I do not have

time for this. I do not have time for this. I do not have time for this. I do not have time for this. I do not have time for this. I do not have time for this. I do not have time for this. I do not have time for this. I do not have time for this. I do not have time for this. I do not have time for this. I do not have time for this. I do not have time for this. I do not have time for this. I do not have time for this. I do not have time for this. I do not have time for this. I do

not have time for this. I do

not have time for this. I do

not have time for this. I do

not have time for this. I do

not have time for this. I do

not have time for this. I do

not have time for this. I do

not have time for this. I do

not have time for this. I do

not have time for this. I do

not have time for this. I do not have time for this. I do not have time for this. I do not have time for this. I do not have time for this. I do not have time for this. I do not have time for this. I do not have time for this. I do not have time for

this. I do not have time for this.

I do not have time for this. I do not have time for this. I do not have time for this. I do not have time for this. I do not have time for this.

I do not have time for this.

I do not have time for this. I do not have time for this. I do not have time for this. I do not have time for this. I do not have time for this. I do not have time for this. I do not have time for this. I do not have time for this. I do not have time for this. I do not have time for this. I do not have time for this. I do not have time for this. I do not have

time for this. I do not have time for this. I do not have time for this. I do not have time for this. I do not have time for this. I do not have time for this. I do not have time for this.

I do not have time for this. I do not have time for this. I do not have time for this. I do not have time for this. I do not have

time for this. I do not have time for this. I do not have time for this. I do not have time for this. I

do not have time for this. I do not have time for this. I do not have time for this. I do not have time for this. I do not have time for this. I do not have time for this. I do not have

time for this. I do not have time for this. I do not have time for this. I do not have time for this. I do not

have time for this. I do not have time for this. I do not have time for this. I do not have time for this. I do not have time for this. I do not have time for this. I do not have time for this.

I do not have time for this. I do not have time for this.

I do not have time for this. I do not have time for

this. I do not have time for this. I do not have time for this. I do not have time for this. I do not have time for this. I do not have time for this. I do not have time for this. I do not have time for this.

I do not have time for this. I do not

have time for this. I do not have time for this. I do not have time for this. I do not have time for this. I do not have time for this. I do not have time for this.

I do not have time for this. I do

not have time for this. I do not have time for this. I do not have time for this. I do not have time for this. I do not have time for this. I do not have time for this.

I do not have time for this. I do not have time for this. I do not have time for

this. I do not have time for this. I do not have time for this. I do not have time for this. I do

not have time for this. I do not have time

for this. I do not have time for this. I do

not have time for this. I do not have time for this. I do not have time for this. I do not have time for this.

I do not have time for this. I do not have time for this. I do not have time for this. I do not have time for this. I do not have time

for this. I do not have time for this. I do not have time for this. I do not have time for this. I do not have time for this. I do not have time for this.

I do not have time for this. I do not have time for this. I do not have time for this. I do not have time for this. I do not have time for this.

I do not have time for this. I do not have time for this. I do not have time for this. I do not have time for this. I do not have time for this.

I do not have time for this. I do not have time for this. I do not have time for this. I do not have time for this.

I do not have time for this. I do not have time for this.

I do not have time for this. I do not have time for this. I do

not have time for this.

I do not have time for this. I do not have time for this. I do not have time for this.

I do not have time for this. I do not have time for this.

I do not have time for this.

I do not have time for this. I do not have time for this.

I do not have time for this. I do not have time for this. I do not have time for this.

I do not have time for this. I do not have time for this. I do not have time for this.

I do not have time for this. I do not have time for this. I do not have time for this. I do not have time for this.

I do not have time for this. I do not have time for

this. I do not have time for this. I do not have time for this. I do not have time for this. I do not have time for this. I do not have time for this. I do not have time for this. I do not have time for this. I do not have time for

this.

I do not have time for this. I do

not have time for this. I do not have time for this. I do not have time for this. I do not have time for this. I do not have time for this. I do not have time for this. I do not have time for this. I do not have time for this. I do not have time

for

this. I do not have time for this.I do not have time for this. I do

not have time for this. I do not have time for this. I do not have time for this. I do not have time for this. I do not have time for this. I do not have time for this. I do not have time for this. I do not have time for this. I do not have

time

for this. I do not have time for this. I do

not have time for this. I do not have time for this. I do not have time for this. I do not have time for this. I do not have time for this. I do not have time for this. I do not have time for this. I do not have time for this. I do not have time for this. I do not have time for this. I do not

have

time for this. I do not have time for this. I do not have

time for this. I do not have time for this. I do not have time for this. I do not have time for this. I do not have time for this. I do not have time for this. I do not have time for this. I do not have time for this. I do not have time for this. I do not have time for this. I do not have time for this. I do

not

have time for this. I do not have time for this. I do

not have time for this. I do not have time for this. I do not have time for this. I do not have time for this. I do not have time for this. I do not have time for this. I do not have time for this. I do not have time for this. I do not have time for this. I do not have time for this. I do not have time for this. I

do

not have time for this. I do not have time for this. I do

not have time for this. I do not have time for this. I do not have time for this. I do not have time for this. I do not have time for this. I do not have time for this. I do not have time for this. I do not have time for this. I do not have time for this. I do not have time for this. I do not have time for this.

I

do not have time for this. I do

not have time for this. I do not have time for this.

I do not have time for this.

I do not have time for this.

I do not have time for this.

I do not have time for this.

I do not have time for this.

I do not have time for this.

I do not have time for this. I do not have time for this. I do not have time for this. I do not have time for this. I do not have time for this.

I do not have time for this. I do not have time for this.

I do not have time for this. I do

not have time for this. I do not have time for this.

I do not have time for this.

I do not have time for this. I do not have time for this. I do not have time for this. I do not have time for this. I do not have time for this. I do not have time for this. I do not have time for this. I do not have time for this. I do not have time for this. I do not have time for this. I do

not have time for this. I do not have time for this. I do not have

time for this. I do not have time for this. I do not have time for this. I do not have time for this. I do not have time for this. I do not have time for this. I do not have time for this.

I do not have time for this. I do not have time for this. I do not have time for this. I do not have time for this. I do not have time for this. I do not have time for this. I do not have time for this. I do not have time for this. I

do

not have

time for

this.

I

do not have time for this. I do not have time for this. I do not have time for this. I do not have time for this. I do not have time for this. I do not have time for this. I do not have

time for this. I do not have time for this. I do not have time for this. I do not have time for this. I do not

have time for this. I do not have time for this. I do not have time for this. I do not have time for this. I do not have time for this. I do not have time for this. I do not have time for this.

I do not have time for this. I do not have time for this. I do not have time for this. I do not have time for this. I do not have time for this. I do not have time for this. I do not have time for this. I do not have time for this. I do not have time for this. I do not have time for this. I do not have time for this. I do not have time for this. I do not have time for this. I do not have time for this.

I do not have time for this. I do not have time for this. I do not have time for this. I do not have time for this. I do not have time for this. I do not have time for this. I do not have time for this. I do not have time for this.

I do not have time for this. I do not have time for this. I do not have time for this. I do not have time for this. I do not have time for this. I do not have time for this. I do not have time for this. I do not have time for this. I do not have time for this. I do not have time for this. I do not have time for this. I do not have time for this. I do not have time for this.

I do not have time for this.

I do not have time for

this. I do not have time

for this. I do not have

time for this. I do not

have time for this. I do

not have time for this. I

do not have time for this. I do not have time

for this. I do not have time for this. I do not have

time for this. I do not have time for this.

I do not have time for this.

I do not have time

for this. I do

not have time for this. I do not have time for this. I do not have time for this. I do not have time for this. I do not have time for this. I do not have time for this. I do not have time for this. I do not have time for this. I do not have time for this. I do not have time for this. I do not have time for this. I do not have time for this. I do not have time for this. I do not have time for this. I do not have time for this. I do not have time for this. I do not have time for this. I do not have time for this. I do

not have time for this. I do not have time for this. I do not have time for this. I do not have time for this. I do not have time for this. I do not have time for this. I do not have time for this.

I do not have time for this. I do not have time for this. I do not have time for this. I do not have time for this. I do not have time for this. I do not have time for this. I do not have time for this. I do not have time for this. I do not have time for this. I do not have time for this. I do not have time for this. I do not have time for this. I do not have time for this. I do not have time for this. I do not have time for this. I do not have time for this. I do not have time for this. I do not have time for this. I do not have time for this. I do not have time for this.

I

do not have

time for this. I do not

have time for this. I do not

have time for this. I do not have

time for this. I do not have time for

this. I do not have time for this. I do not have

time for this. I do not have time for this. I do not have

time for this. I do not have time for this. I do not have

time for this. I do not have time for this. I do not have time for this. I do not have time for this. I do not have time for this. I do not have time for this. I do not have time for this. I do not have time for this. I do not have time for this. I do not have time for this.

I do not have time for this. I do

not have time for this. I do not

have time for this. I do not

have time for this. I do

not have time for this.

I do not have

time for

this.

I do not have time for this. I do

not have time for this. I do not have time for this. I do not have time for this. I do not have time for this. I do not have time for this. I do not have time for this. I do not have time for this. I do not have time for this. I do not have time for this. I do not have time for this. I do not have time for this. I do not have time for this. I do not have time for this. I do not have time for this. I do not have time for this. I do not have time for this. I do not have time for this. I do not have time for this.

I do not have time for this.

I do not have time for this. I do not have time for this.

I do not have time for this. I do not have time for this.

I do not have time for this. I do not have time for this. I do not have time for this. I do not have time for this. I do not have time for this. I do not have time for this. I do not have time for this. I do not have time for this. I do not have time for this. I do not have time for this. I do not have time for this. I do not have time for this. I do not have time for this. I do not have time for this. I do not have time for

this. I do not have time for this. I do not have time for this. I do not have time for this. I do not have time for this. I do not have time for this. I do not have time for this. I do not have time for this.

I d

o n

ot h

av

e t

im

e f

or th

is.

I

do

no

t

ha

ve

ti

me

fo

r

t

hi

s.

I do not have time for this. I do not have time for this. I do not have time for this. I do not have time for this. I do not have time for this. I do not have time for this.

I do not have time for this. I do not have time for this.

I do not have time for this. I do not have time for this. I do

not have time for this. I do not have time for this. I do

not have time for this. I do not have time for this. I do not have time for this. I do not have time for this. I do not have time for this.

I do not have time for this. I do not have time for this.

I do

not have

time for

this.

I do not have time for this. I do not have time for this. I do not have time for this. I do not have time for this. I do not have time for this. I do not have time for this. I do not have time for this. I do not have time for this. I do not have time for this. I do not have time for this. I do not have time for this. I do not have

time for this. I do not have time for this.

I do not have time for this. I do not have

time for this. I do not have time for this. I didn’t ask for this.

I didn’t ask for this.

I do not have time for this. I do not have time for this. I do not have time for this. I do not have time for this. I do not have time for this. I do not have time for this. I do not have time for this. I do not have time for this. I do not have time for this. I do not have time for this. I do not have time for this. I do not have time for this. I do not have time for this. I do not have time for this. I do not have time for this. I do not have time for this. I do not have time for this. I do not have time for this. I do not have time for this. I do

not have time for this. I do not have time for this. I do not have time for this. I do not have time for this. I do not have time for this. I do not have time for this. I do not have time for this. I do not have time for this. I do not have time for this.

I do not have time for this.

I do not have time for this. I do not have time for this.

I do not have time for this. I do not have time for this. I do not have time for this.

I do not have time for this. I do not have time for this. I do not have time for this. I do not have time for this.

I do not have time for this. I do not have time for this. I do not have time for this. I do not have time for this. I do not have time for this.

I do not have time for this. I do not have time for this. I do not have time for this. I do not have time for this. I do not have time for this. I do not have time for this.

I definitely do not have time for this.

I definitely do not have time for this.

I definitely do not have time for this.

I definitely do not have time for this.

I do not have time for this. I do not have time for this.

I do not have time for this. I do not have time for this. I do not have time for this. I do not have time for this. I do not have time for this. I do not have time for this. I do not have time for this.

I do not have time for this. I do not have time for this.

I do not have time for this. I do not have time for this. I do not have time for this.

I do not have time for this. I do not have time for this. I do not have time for this. I do not have time for this. I do not have time for this. I do not have time for this. I do not have time for this. I do not have time for this. I do not have time for this. I do not have time for this. I do not have time for this. I do not have time for this. I do not have time for this. I do not have time for this. I do not have time for this. I do not have time for this. I do not have time for this. I do not have time for this.

I do not have time for this.

I do not have time for this.

I do not have time for this. I do not have time for this.

I do not have time for this. I do not have time for this. I do not have time for this. I do not have time for this. I didn't ask for this.

I do not have time for this. I do not have time for this. I do not have time for this. I do not have time for this. I do not have time for this. I do not have time for this. I do not have time for this. I do not have time for this. I do not have time for this. I do not have time for this. I do not have time for this. I do not have time for this. I do not have time for this. I do not have time for this.

I do not have time for this. I do not have time for this. I do not have time for this. I do not have time for this. I do not have time for this. I do not have time for this. I do not have time for this. I do not have time for this. I do not have time for this. I do not have time for this. I do not have time for this. I do not have time for this.

I do not have time for this. I do not have time for this. I do not have time for this. I do not have time for this. I do not have time for this. I do not have time for this. I do not have time for this.

I do not have time for this. I do not have time for this. I do not have time for this. I do not have time for this. I do not have

time for this. I do not have time for this.

I do not have time for this.

I do not

have time for this. I do not

have time for this. I do not have time for this.

I do not have time for this. I do not have time for this. I do not have time for this. I do not have time for this. I do not have

time for this. I do not have time for this. I do not have time for this. I do not have time for this. I do not have time for this. I do not have time for this. I do not have time for this. I do not have time for this. I do not have time for this. I do not have

time for this. I do not have time for this. I do not have time for this. I do not have time for this. I do not have time for this.

I do not have time for this. I do not have time for this. I do not have time for this. I do not have time for this. I

do not have time for this. I do not have time for this. I do

not have time for this. I do not have ti

me for this.

I do not have time for this.

I do not have time for this. I do not have time for this. I do not have time for this. I do not have time for this. I do not have time for this.

I do not have time for this. I do not have time for this. I do not have time for this. I do not have time for this.

I do not have time for this. I do not have time for this.

I do not have time for this. I do not have time for this. I do not have time for this. I do not have time for this. I do not have time for this. I do not have time for this.

I do not have time for this. I do not have time for this.

I do not have time for this.

I do not have time for this.

I do not have time for this. I do not have time for this.

I do not have

time for

this.

I do not

have time for

this. I do not have time

for this. I do not have time for this. I do not have time for this. I do not have time for this. I do not have time for this. I do not have time for this. I do not have time for this. I do not have time for this. I do not have time for this. I do not have time for this. I do not have time for this. I do not have time for this. I do not have time for this. I do not have time for this. I do not have time for this. I do not have time for this. I do not have time for this. I do not have time for this. I do not have time for this. I do

not have time for this. I do not have time for this. I do not have time for this. I do not have time for this. I do not have time for this. I do not have time for this. I do not have time for this. I do not have time for this. I do not have time for this. I do not have time for this. I do not have time for this. I do not have time for this. I do

not

have time for this.

I do not have time for this. I do not

have time for this. I do not have time for this. I do not

have time for this. I do not have time for this.

I do not have time for this. I do not have time for

this. I do not have time for this. I do not

have time for this. I do not

have

time for this. I do not have time for this. I do not have time for this. I do not have time for this. I do not have time for this. I do not have time for this. I do not have

time for this. I do not have time for this. I do not have time for this. I do not have time for this. I do not have time for this. I do not have time for this. I do not have time for this.

I do not have time for this. I do not have time for this. I do not have time for this. I do not have time for this. I do not have time for this. I do not have time for this. I do not have time for this. I do not have time for this. I do not have time for this. I

do not have time for this. I do not have time for this. I do not have time for this. I do not have time for this. I do not have time for this. I do not have time for this. I do not have

time for this. I do not have time for this. I do not have time for this. I do not have time for this. I do not

have time for this.

I do not have time for this. I do not have time for this.

I do not have time for this.

I do not have time for this. I do not have time for this.

I do not have time for this.

I do not have time for this. I do not have time for this.

I do not have time for this.

I do not have time for this. I do not have time for this.

I do not have time for this.

I do not have time for this. I do not have time for this.

I do not have time for this.

I do not have time for this. I do not have time for this.

I do not have time for this.

I do not have time for this. I do not have time for this.

I do not have time for this.

I do not have time for this. I do not have time for this.

I do not have time for this. I do not have time for this. I do not have time for this. I do not have time for this. I do not have time for this.

I do not have time for this. I do not have time for this. I do not have time for this.

I do not have time for this.

I do not have time for this. I do not have time for this. I do not have time for this.

I do not have time for this.

I do not have time for this. I do not have time for this. I do not have time for this.

I do not have time for this.

I do not have time for this. I do not have time for this. I do not have time for this.

I do not have time for this.

I do not have time for this. I do not have time for this. I do not have time for this.

I do not have time for this.

I do not have time for this. I do not have time for this. I do not have time for this.

I do not have time for this.

I do not have time for this. I do not have time for this.

I do not have time for this. I do not have time for this. I do not have time for this.

I do not have time for this. I do not have time for this.

I do not have time for this. I do not have time for this. I do not have time for this.

I do not have time for this. I do not have time for this.

I do not have time for this. I do not have time for this. I do

not have time for this.

I do not have time for this. I do not have time for this.

I do not have time for this. I do not have time for this. I do not have time for this.

I do not have time for this. I do not have time for this.

I do not have time for this. I do not have time for this. I do not have time for this.

I do not have time for this. I do not have time for this.

I do not have time for this. I do not have time for this. I do not have time for this.

I do not have time for this. I do not have time for this.

I do not have time for this. I do not have time for this. I do not have time for this. I do not have time for this. I do not have time for this. I do not have time for this. I do not have time for this. I do not have time for this. I do not have time for this. I do not have time for this. I do not have time for this. I do not have time for this. I do not have time for this. I do not have time for this. I do not have time for this. I do not have time for this.

I do not have time for this. I do not have time for this. I do not have time for this.

I do not have time for this. I do not have time for this. I do not have time for this. I do not have time for this. I do not have

time for this. I do not have time for this. I do not have time for this. I do not have time for this. I do not have time for this. I do not have time for this. I do not have time for this. I do not have time for this. I do not have time for this. I do not have time for this. I do not have time for this. I do not have time for this. I do not have time for this. I do not have time for this. I do not have time for this.

I do not have time for this. I do not have time for this. I do not have time for this. I do not have time for this. I do not have time for this. I do not have time for this. I do not have time for this. I do not have time for this. I do not have time for this. I do not have time for this. I do not have time for this. I do not have time for this. I do not have time for this.

I do not have time for this. I do not have time for this. I do not have time for this. I do not have time for this. I do not have time for this. I do not have time for this. I do not have time for this. I do not have time for this. I do not have time for this. I do not have time for this. I do not have time for this.

I do not have time for this. I do not have time for this. I do not have time for this. I do not have time for this. I do not have time for this. I do not have time for this. I do not have time for this. I do not have time for this. I do not have time for this. I do not have time for this.

I do not have time for this. I do not have time for this. I do not have time for this. I do not have time for this. I do not have time for this. I do not have time for this. I do not have time for this. I do not have time for this. I do not have time for this.

I do not have time for this. I do not have time for this. I do not have time for this. I do not have time for this. I do not have time for this. I do not have time for this. I do not have time for this. I do not have time for this.

I do not have time for this. I do not have time for this. I do not have time for this. I do not have time for this. I do not have time for this. I do not have time for this. I do not have time for this.

I do not have time for this. I do not have time for this. I do not have time for this. I do not have time for this. I do not have time for this.

I do not have time for this. I do not have time for this. I do not have time for this. I do not have time for this.

I do not have time for this. I do not have time for this. I do not have time for this.

I do not have time for this. I do not have time for this.

I do not have time for this.

I do not have time for this.

I do not have time for this.

I do not have time for this.

I do not have time for this.

I do not have time for this.

I do not have time for this.

I do not have time for this.

I do not have time for this. I do

not have time for this. I do not have time for this. I do

not have time for this. I do not have time for this. I do

not have time for this. I do not have time for this. I do

not have time for this. I do not have time for this.

I do not have time for this.

ABOUT THE AUTHOR

Forbes 30 Under 30, James Earl Cox III completed a self-set challenge of making 100 games in 5 years. Co-founder of Seemingly Pointless, he holds a master's degree from the University of Southern California in Interactive Media and Game Design and is a Miami University of Ohio alumnus, with honors, in Creative Writing, Mass Communication, and Interactive Media. His work has been exhibited at E3, Slamdance Film Festival, Fantastic Arcade, was a finalist in the IGF, received awards from IndieCade, Serious Play, Meaningful Play, and has been displayed in the Smithsonian Pop-Up Arcade as well as in The National Art Center, Tokyo. His work can be found at Just404it.com and SeeminglyPointless.com.